EXPO

International Expositions 1851–2010

D0851196

EXPO

International Expositions 1851–2010

Anna Jackson

V&A Publishing

First published by V&A Publishing, 2008
V&A Publishing
Victoria and Albert Museum
South Kensington
London SW7 2RL

Distributed in North America by Harry N. Abrams, Inc., New York

Paperback edition
ISBN 978 1 85177 540 8
Library of Congress Control Number 2008922657

10 9 8 7 6 5 4 3 2 1
2012 2011 2010 2009 2008

A catalogue record for this book is available from the British Library.

Designer: Andrew Shoolbred
Copy-editor: Delia Gaze
Indexer: Christine Shuttleworth

New V&A photography by Ken Jackson, V&A Photographic Studio

Printed in Italy

Front cover illustrations: Details of plates 97,17, 50, 92, 2, 33 and 98
Back cover illustrations: Details of plates 85, 5, 61, 90 and 45

Page 3: Details of plates 2, 49, 78, 98
Page 9: Details of plates 17, 12, 2, 22, 20 and 5
Page 41: Details of plates 45, 32, 27, 50, 33 and 49
Page 67: Details of plates 56, 78, 69, 61 and 76
Page 91: Details of plates 85, 81, 90, 97, 92 and 98

V&A Publishing
Victoria and Albert Museum
South Kensington
London SW7 2RL
www.vam.ac.uk

PREFACE

ACKNOWLEDGEMENTS

This book has been produced to accompany a travelling exhibition, *Expo x Expo: World Expos from 1851–2010,* organized by the Bureau International des Expositions. It has been a pleasure to collaborate with the BIE on this exciting project and I would particularly like to thank Vicente Gonzalez Loscertales and Dimitri Kerkentzes for all their help and support and the generous contribution of the three expositions, Aichi 2005, Zaragoza 2008 and Shanghai 2010.

The publication would not have been possible without the assistance of Yueh-Siang Chang who has worked enthusiastically and tirelessly on the project, helping with research, sourcing the images and compiling the chronology. I am also very grateful to my colleagues in the Asian Department, particularly Dominica Blenkinsopp and Beth McKillop, and to other colleagues in the Victoria and Albert Museum. The staff of the Word and Image Department, particularly Robin Crawford, Leon Leigh and Deborah Sutherland of the National Art Library, have been extremely helpful; Sophie Connor spent many hours carefully conserving the 1851 panorama; Ken Jackson and Paul Robins in the Photographic Studio created the wonderful images; and the Publishing Department, especially Monica Woods, guided the book through to production. I would also like to thank Delia Gaze for her meticulous editing and Andrew Shoolbred for the beautiful design.

I would also like to extend my gratitude to Dominique Lobstein and Caroline Mathieu at the Musée d'Orsay, Claude Billaud and Jean-Paul Avice at the Bibliothèque historique de la ville de Paris, and colleagues at the Wolfsonian-Florida International University, Miami Beach, and the National Museum of American History, Smithsonian Institution, Washington, DC, particularly Susan Strange in the Archives Center.

I am indebted to Jane Pavitt, Jana Scholze and David Crowley, for so generously sharing their knowledge of postwar expositions, and I would also like to thank the many other friends and colleagues who have provided help and support: Martin Barnes, William Coaldrake, Laura Frampton, Tom Genova, Jonathan King, Karen Livingstone, Geoffrey Marsh, Peter Martin, Laura Schiavo, Jonathan Sweet, Akiko Terao and Ghislaine Wood.

Most of all I would like to thank Paul Greenhalgh, Director of the Corcoran Museum in Washington, with whom I have shared exposition ideas over the many years of our friendship, and Mark Jones, Director of the V&A, who initiated this project and has provided continual guidance, support and encouragement.

PREFACE

Fairs are as old as human civilization. People come together to trade objects and information, to learn from others and to show off. They define, even create, supra-communities, wider than family or village, city or even state. What is remarkable about international expositions, or world's fairs, is that they were the first events to envisage the whole world as a single community. They mark the moment at which it became possible to conceive of humanity united by a single interest and the globe represented in all its magnificent variety in a single place.

The *Great Exhibition of the Works of Industry of All Nations* of 1851 was the first occasion on which the world looked at itself in this new way. It and subsequent expositions were seen as beacons of hope for peace based on the exchange of goods and ideas; but they also spurred intense rivalry, competitive display and the desire for progress. By bringing commodities, cultures and ideas from every part of the earth to one place, they seemed to make the world smaller; but the increasing scale and ambition of successive expositions also revealed its vastness and diversity. They evidenced the stability of a system that could organize so complex an event and yet they offered a dizzying glimpse of future change.

Expositions have done many things. They have celebrated national pride and international solidarity; they have expressed the quintessence of each generation's understanding of its past and consistently aimed to select and display the best of the present. But it is their role in imagining the future that is most significant. New ideas about how to live, new concepts of urban design, new technologies of all kinds have begun their road to acceptance in successive world expos. Recent expositions continue this tradition and I predict that Shanghai 2010 will reveal to all its tens of millions of visitors a startling new vision of the world to come.

MARK JONES
Director, Victoria and Albert Museum

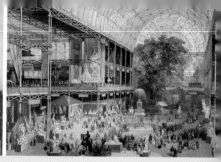

THE WORLD'S STAGE

I wish you *could* have witnessed the *1st May* 1851, the *greatest* day in
our history, and the most *beautiful* and *imposing* and *touching* spectacle
ever seen, and the triumph of my beloved Albert. Truly it was astonishing,
a fairy scene . . . It was the *happiest, proudest* day in my life, and I can
think of nothing else.

QUEEN VICTORIA[1]

So wrote Queen Victoria to Leopold I, King of the Belgians, two days after she had opened the *Great Exhibition of the Works of Industry of All Nations* in London (pl. 1). More than 650,000 people had cheered the royal procession as it made its way to Hyde Park, while 25,000 visitors filled the specially constructed exhibition building, named the Crystal Palace by *Punch* magazine. Inside this remarkable iron and glass structure 14,000 exhibitors displayed more than 100,000 exhibits from Britain and around the world.[2] The vast spectacle, of which the crowds themselves were part, created a sense of wonder and amazement, a feeling – as Victoria herself had noted – of being in a fairy tale (pl. 2). By the time the doors of the Crystal Palace closed on 11 October, 6,039,195 people had paid to see the exhibition.[3]

The Great Exhibition was a landmark event, its enormous success inspiring immediate imitators in New York and Dublin in 1853. It was in Paris in 1855, however, that the next major international exhibition was held, and from there the genre spread around the globe. The great exhibitions, expositions and world's fairs that have taken place since 1851 rank among the most spectacular, popular and important events ever staged. Unsurpassed in their scale and confidence, the expositions have been encyclopedic endeavours, offering explanations of the past and predictions of the future. The greatest gatherings of people in times of peace, they have educated and entertained millions through the presentation of the very latest developments in art, science and technology from around the world, displayed in a fabulous array of buildings and parks. Expositions are ephemeral events lasting six months at most, yet their impact has been long lasting and profound. They have exerted enormous influence on developments in architecture and urban planning, transportation, mass communication, consumerism, science, technology, art, industrial design, popular culture, entertainment and leisure. Most of all, they have affected how people have understood the world and their part in it. Expositions have shaped the modern world, and made that modernity manifest.

People have gathered at fairs for purposes of commerce and pleasure since antiquity. The real precedents for the Great Exhibition, however, were the French national exhibitions of industrial and craft products staged in the post-revolution period to stimulate trade and manufacture. Ten of these were held between 1798 and 1849, each building on the size and ambitions of its predecessor. In Britain, too, from 1760 exhibitions of art and industry were staged by the Society of Arts.[4] These were much smaller than the

French events and were held less to stimulate the economy than to enlighten manufacturers and business leaders. From the 1840s the Mechanics Institute, inspired by the example of the Society of Arts, also began to hold large displays with the aim of educating the working classes.

The French and British exhibitions were increasingly successful, but were limited to showing the products of the host nation. In France as early as the 1830s the staging of an international exhibition had been suggested, but fear of foreign competition had quashed the idea. The concept was circulated again in 1849, however, when it came to the attention of Henry Cole, one of

1
The Opening of the Great Exhibition by Queen Victoria on 1st May 1851, Henry Courtney Selous. Oil on canvas, 1851–2.
V&A: 323–1889

2
*The Transept from the Grand
Entrance, Souvenir of the
Great Exhibition*, J. McNeven.
Colour lithograph, 1851.
V&A: 19627

the British visitors to the French exhibition and the man who was to be the chief organizer of the Great Exhibition. Cole, who was Assistant Keeper of the Public Records Office, was a great advocate of free trade, believing that the lifting of government restrictions on the flow of goods would usher in an era of peace and prosperity for all. On returning to London he put his ideas to Prince Albert, Queen Victoria's husband and President of the, now Royal, Society of Arts, which at this point was planning its next exhibition. The Prince Consort responded positively to Cole, declaring that the exhibition 'must embrace foreign productions'.[5] Thus the international exposition was born, with 32 foreign countries participating in the event of 1851.[6] The exhibition was organized by a Royal Commission, of which Prince Albert was Honorary President, and financed through a network of 300 local committees, which were responsible for raising funds and encouraging participation.

The Great Exhibition is often viewed as a supreme symbol of Britain's mid-nineteenth-century confidence as the world's leading industrial nation. The state of the economy, however, was far from robust in the 'hungry forties'.[7] There was also a widespread concern that the country's system of industrial education was inadequate and that the production of goods that could perform well in domestic and foreign markets was suffering as a consequence. The exhibition therefore was aimed as much at solving some of Britain's industrial problems as at celebrating its successes. This was also a period of political and social unrest, the year 1848 witnessing Chartist demonstrations in Britain and revolution across Europe. Indeed, opposition to holding an international exhibition came primarily from those who feared that the event would attract socialist agitators and foreign refugees, as well as thieves and vagrants. The predicted hoards of rogues and revolutionaries failed to materialize, however, and the exhibition passed off peacefully. The potential behaviour of the artisan classes who were able, after 26 May, to enter the exhibition for a shilling on Mondays to Thursdays was also a cause for concern, but they remained as well behaved and enthralled by what they saw as those who had paid more for admission (pl. 3).

The overriding aim of the Great Exhibition was to educate the populace about the value of industry and commerce and thus to stimulate trade. These themes, of education and trade, were to become cornerstones of the rhetoric that drove and justified the planning and realization of the international expositions through much of their subsequent history, despite the tremendous differences in the social, economic and political contexts in which they were staged.[8] The other enduring elements of the conceptual framework of expositions were first expressed in a speech that Prince Albert made in 1850 as the Great Exhibition was being planned:

> Nobody who has paid any attention to the particular features of our present era, will doubt for a moment that we are living in a period of the most wonderful transition, which tends rapidly to the accomplishment of that great end to which, indeed, all history points – the realisation of the unity of mankind . . . The exhibition of 1851 is to give us a true test and living picture of the point of development at which the whole of mankind

has arrived in this great task, and a new starting point from which all nations will be able to direct their further exertions. I confidently hope that . . . this vast collection will produce upon the spectator . . . the conviction that these [blessings of the Almighty] can only be realised in proportion to the help which we are prepared to render to each other – therefore, only by peace, love, and ready assistance, not only between individuals, but between the nations of the earth.[9]

Peace and progress became the great mantras of expositions. These events were born of a conviction that humanity would improve through international cooperation, and that the coming together of people to show the achievements of their respective countries and cultures would lead to a fellowship of man. The expression of this belief has remained remarkably constant throughout the history of expositions, despite the fact that many events have been staged at times of conflict and the true impetus for participation has often been international rivalry, not harmony. More than anything else, international expositions were conceived and perceived as the visible manifestation of the notion of progress. They were staged not only to reveal the achievements of the present, but also to suggest that civilization was advancing towards a utopian future. The primary vehicle for the achievement of this goal was technology, which, in the nineteenth century, was linked to Darwinian notions of evolution, making progress an inevitable and unstoppable force for good.[10] Technological progress, it was believed, would transform the world and lead inevitably to social progress and a better life for all mankind.

The organizers of the early expositions realized, however, that people

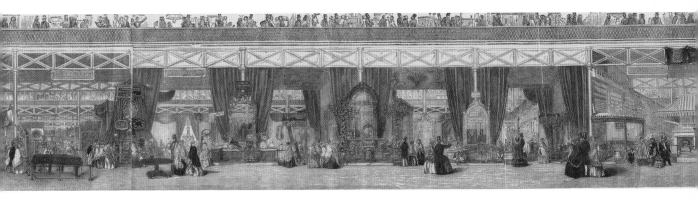

required explanation and reassurance in the face of such rapid 'progress'. These events provided a means by which the public could be acquainted with, and reconciled to, the social and psychological changes that increasing industrialization and globalization would bring. The expositions proved to be powerful mediums for conveying complex ideas, the physical and visual immediacy of the displays making the whole world seem comprehensible. The particular vision of the world on display was, however, the creation of small, powerful elites who used the expositions to consolidate their political and economic authority. As such, these events were successful agents of propaganda; they influenced individual and collective values and beliefs enormously and helped to build in those who visited them a powerful sense of modern identity and culture.[11]

The Great Exhibition was global in outlook, revealing to the world Britain's industrial leadership. Yet its focus was also national, since it was designed to impress upon the British people the extent of the country's power and to instil in them a sense of nationhood. These two apparently contradictory, but inextricably linked aspects of expositions – nationalism and internationalism – were at the heart of Napoleon III's plans for the *Exposition Universelle* of 1855. The staging of the exposition was part of a determined policy to lend legitimacy and prestige to the Second Empire.[12] Funded by public money and organized by the emperor's cousin Prince Napoleon, it aimed to demonstrate to the French people, and to France's allies and enemies, the power and spirit of the Napoleonic legacy. The exhibition trumpeted the country's cultural and artistic supremacy, while projecting an image of a progressive industrial state.

3
Detail of the *Grand Panorama of the Great Exhibition of All Nations 1851*. Wood-engraving coloured by hand. Published by the *Illustrated London News*, 1852.
V&A: NAL

In his inaugural speech at the Palais de l'Industrie, Napoleon III proclaimed that it was with great happiness that he opened 'this temple of peace that brings together all peoples in a spirit of concord'.[13] This optimistic exposition rhetoric seemed blatantly to contradict the reality of the day, for as the emperor made his speech French troops were fighting alongside the British against Russia in the Crimean War. Yet the military victories won by the allies served only to enhance Napoleon's international status and bolster national pride, lending his exposition a triumphant air. The alliance between France and Britain was important to Napoleon and, although he hoped to equal the success of the Great Exhibition, he avoided any hint of international rivalry. The emperor's success was sealed, and the lingering antagonisms of the Napoleonic wars swept aside, when Queen Victoria was welcomed by a great crowd as she visited the *Exposition Universelle*, the first time a reigning monarch of England had visited the French capital since 1431.

The expositions baton was passed back to Britain, which staged the next international exhibition in 1862. The event was bigger than that of 1851, but it was not such a success, existing as it did in the shadows cast by the Great Exhibition and by the death of Prince Albert in December 1861. The *London International Exhibition* of 1862 was to be Britain's last great international exhibition, although London hosted a series of events in the 1870s, and Edinburgh and Glasgow also staged important exhibitions.[14] If it was the Great Exhibition that established the model by which international expositions were

4
Dispositions intérieures du Palais de l'Exposition, Deroy fils et Jacob. Engraving. 1867.
MUSEE CARNAVALET, PARIS.
© ROGER-VIOLLET

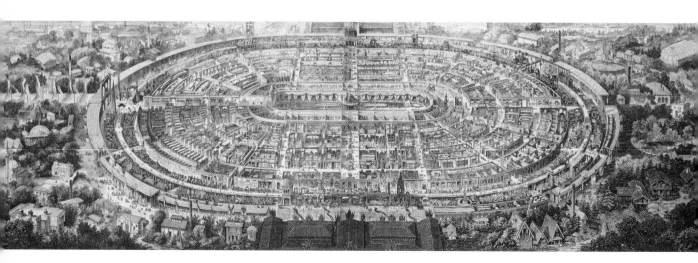

first judged, it was the Parisian events that raised those standards to new heights. Between 1855 and 1900 the French capital hosted five *Expositions Universelles*, each more flamboyant than the one before.

In hosting a second exhibition in Paris in 1867, Napoleon III sought to position the French capital as the centre of world civilization. The emperor enlisted some of France's leading artists and thinkers to help proclaim this message. They included Victor Hugo, who declared such lofty aspirations in his introduction to the *Paris Guide*:

> O France, adieu! Thou art too great to remain merely a fatherland. To become a goddess, thou must be separated from motherhood . . . Thou shall no longer be France: thou shall be Humanity! No longer a nation thou shall be Ubiquity! . . . and as Athens became Greece, as Rome became Christianity, thou, France, become the world! [15]

The general commissioner for the exposition of 1867, Frédéric Le Play, was also driven by a utopian vision. His was based on the notion that every aspect of human activity should be imbued with moral purpose and that traditional social values could be allied with modern technology and the international exchange of products and knowledge to bring about universal harmony for the human race.[16] The main exhibition building on the Champ de Mars was conceived as a vast encyclopedia in which visitors would be presented with every facet of human endeavour.[17] It was an immense iron and glass ellipse, a mile in circumference, with concentric zones that housed similar products and radiating sections that were given over to particular countries – by moving along the circles visitors could see a particular branch of industry and by moving in and out along radials they could see all the products of one country (pl. 4). In practice, this system did not always work, for not all countries were able to fill their slice of the 'cake', and there were complaints that the continual curve of the building was rather fatiguing on the eye. But the design of the Palais de Champ de Mars did represent a real attempt to classify a bewildering variety of products in a meaningful and didactic way, and to create a panorama of mankind's achievements.[18]

The innermost ring of the Palais contained a special exhibit, the *Histoire du Travail*, which showed the advances of the human race since the Stone Age, the first theme display in an exposition. The event of 1867 was innovative in other ways. Visitors could take a sightseeing boat trip along the Seine and

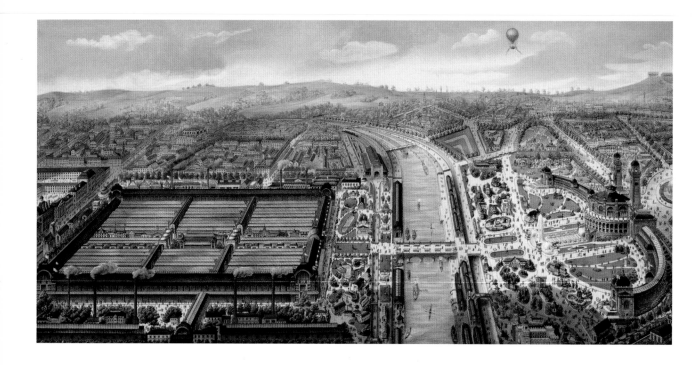

5

Exposition universelle de 1878: panorama des palais et jardins du Champ de Mars, Cheveneau. Colour lithograph. 1878.

© MUSEE DE L'AIR ET DE L'ESPACE, PARIS

To the right can be seen the new Palais de Trocadéro and on the left the Palais de l'Industrie, with the Rue de Nations running down the central courtyard.

enjoy the park outside the main building, which stayed open until 11 o'clock in the evening and contained a series of international restaurants and pavilions erected by participating countries.[19] Here visitors could wander among such diverse attractions as a mosque, a Tunisian palace, a Swiss chalet, a replica of the temple of Philae and a Gothic cathedral. It was the pleasures of this park, rather than the didactic content of the exhibition building, that proved most popular with visitors, providing a model for future expositions.[20]

One of the most popular displays at the 1867 exposition was the gigantic 14-inch (35.6 m) gun presented by Alfred Krupp (see pl. 82). Ironically, it was Krupp's canons that served the Prussians so effectively in their defeat of the French in 1870 and which bombarded Paris in the subsequent siege of the capital.[21] The next exposition staged by France, in 1878, was an attempt by the Third Republic to transcend such painful memories of the Franco-Prussian War and the Commune and to reveal to the world that France was ready yet again to assume its role as the world's great civilizer. This event spread beyond the boundaries of the Champ de Mars, across the Seine and up the hill to the newly constructed Palais de Trocadéro, which housed a concert hall and a

6
*Vue générale de l'Exposition
universelle de Paris 1889,*
Servando. Colour lithograph. 1889.
MUSEE CARNAVALET, PARIS.
© PHOTO RMN – BULLOZ

The Eiffel Tower stands between the
Galerie des Machines, on the left, and
the Palais de Trocadéro on the other
side of the Seine.

retrospective exhibition of decorative art (pl. 5). The rooms of the Trocadéro
were also the venues for a number of international conferences and con-
gresses, which were important features of the early expositions. In 1878
discussions held at the Congress for the Protection of Literary Property
eventually led to the formulation of international copyright laws, while
the International Congress for the Amelioration of the Condition of Blind
People resulted in the adoption of the Braille system of touch-reading.[22]

The *Exposition Universelle* of 1878 was visited by more than 16 million
people and did much to restore France's international prestige and national
pride, but financially the event was a failure. While the exposition of 1867 had
produced a profit of almost 3 million francs, that of 1878 had lost more than
30 million. This problem weighed heavily on the minds of the organizers of
the next Parisian exposition in 1889, and as a result the government, who
had borne the costs of the previous events, provided only about a third of the
funding, much of the rest being guaranteed by banks. The 1880s were years
of political crisis in France, and the exhibition aimed to provide a boost to the
ailing economy and an opportunity to display the achievements, and affirm
the liberal policies, of the Third Republic. The event of 1889 was staged
to commemorate the centenary of the storming of the Bastille, something

7
The Arab house in the *Histoire de l'Habitation* display at the Paris Exposition of 1889.

that caused great concern to the monarchs of Europe, who had no wish to participate in an event that celebrated revolution. Many countries, including Britain, stayed away, officially at least.

Despite the problems and feelings of disquiet that attended the planning of the *Exposition Universelle* of 1889, the event itself was an enormous success (pl. 6). It was attended by 32 million people and made a tidy profit of 8 million francs. The exposition is best remembered for its two great architectural triumphs, the Galerie des Machines and the Eiffel Tower, but situated at the base of the latter was another remarkable display, the *Histoire de l'Habitation Humaine*, created by Charles Garnier (pl. 7).[23] In the same vein as the *Histoire du Travail* exhibit of 1867, this attempted comprehensiveness, a taxonomy of human dwellings from the prehistoric to the present and including all major world cultures. The houses were slightly smaller than real life, but were constructed with authentic materials and meticulously detailed inside and out.

Also of significance at the Paris Exposition of 1889 were the large colonial displays. The display of empire was central to the international expositions. The presentation of British imperial possessions at the Great

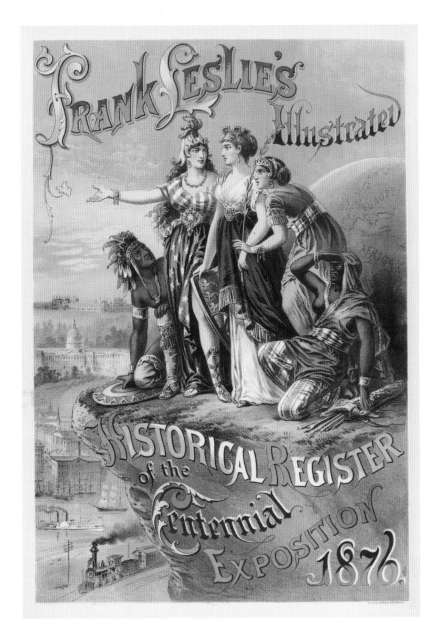

8
Frontispiece from
*Frank Leslie's Illustrated
Historical Register of the
Centennial Exposition, 1876.*
Philadelphia, 1877.

V&A: NAL 54.C.33

The allegorical figure of America is showing the achievements of her nation to Europe, Asia and Africa, while to her right is a Native American. The perceived hierarchy of the different races is revealed in the relative positions of the figures.

Exhibition was designed not only to show the world that Britain controlled much of it, but also to educate the populace on the merits of empire and thus gain support for policies abroad. In 1855 France, alongside other nations, proudly displayed the products of its colonial empire. Such displays grew in size and significance, until by 1889 a whole town of imperial pavilions occupied more than 40 hectares between the Champ de Mars and the Trocadéro, and for the first time Asian and African peoples were displayed in native villages.[24]

9

OPPOSITE: *Obelisk and Grand Vista North from the Colonnade*, from *Jackson's Famous Pictures of the World's Fair*. Chicago, 1895.

V&A: NAL 52.D.135

The inscription on the base of the obelisk reads: 'Four hundred years after the discovery of this continent by Christopher Columbus the nations of the world unite on this spot to compare in friendly emulation their achievements in art science manufactures and agriculture'. To the right is the Machinery Building, with the Electricity Building in the background, and to the left are the Agriculture Building and the vast Manufacturers and Liberal Arts Building.

Many in France had been wary of holding an exposition in 1889 because of the sheer number of other events taking place around the globe, which, they feared, would detract attention from, and participation in, the Parisian event. Expositions were now being held somewhere in the world virtually every year. In the run-up to 1889 events took place in Amsterdam (1883), Calcutta (1883–4), Antwerp (1885), Edinburgh (1886), Barcelona (1888), Glasgow (1888), Brussels (1888) and Melbourne (1888–9).[25] The Parisian expositions remained the standard by which any other event was measured, but in the late nineteenth century the United States began to rival France, at least in terms of monumentality. The first international exposition in America was held in Philadelphia in 1876 and marked the centenary of Independence. As at the European expositions, issues of internationalism and nationalism were of major concern. The *Centennial Exhibition* was staged to demonstrate to the rest of the world that the United States was able to take its place alongside the most advanced nations of Europe (pl. 8). Held only eleven years after the divisive Civil War, it also aimed to instil a sense of national identity in its citizens. The official literature of the exhibition extolled the virtues of the pioneer spirit, republicanism, democracy and progress, aspects of American-ness that would be in evidence in all future fairs held in the United States.[26]

The Philadelphia exhibition was held in several major buildings and smaller pavilions within a landscaped park. As such, it signalled a move away from the established exposition tradition of placing most of the displays in one main building. The increasing importance of the appearance of the exposition site was revealed in the next American event, which was held in Chicago in 1893. This featured an elaborate landscape based around a specially created lagoon and waterways, which provided the setting for 14 main exhibition buildings, all in classical style, and a series of monumental sculptures (pl. 9). Staged to mark the 400th anniversary of Columbus' voyage and to reveal America's technological and cultural prowess, the *World's Columbian Exposition* was hugely successful.[27] On 9 October, Chicago Day, 751,026 people visited the exhibition, the greatest number of people who had ever gathered in one place (pl. 10).

The exhibition in Chicago was the first to have a dedicated entertainment area, the Midway Plaisance, which contained an amazing mixture of sideshows, pleasure rides, troupes of actors and musicians, villages of native peoples, bars and restaurants. This was the major legacy of the Columbian

10
Chicago Day, from *Jackson's Famous Pictures of the World's Fair*. Chicago, 1895.
V&A: NAL 52.D.135

Crowds gather around the Grand Plaza bandstand with the Agriculture Building rising up behind. To the right of the bandstand is the Columbian fountain.

exhibition in terms of exposition history, but its impact on American culture and society was even more profound. The exhibition was supported and financed by a small group of rich businessmen, marking the rise to power of corporations and their wealthy leaders. As the country shifted from an agrarian to an industrialized economy, the technological displays were seen to herald a new age of American progress. Most of all, in inspiring in visitors the desire to purchase all that it had to offer, the exhibition marked the advent of a consumer-based society.

Walter Benjamin famously stated that world expositions were 'places of pilgrimage to the commodity fetish'.[28] The connection between expositions and the commodification of industrial products is certainly a very strong one. The Great Exhibition of 1851, in which manufactured goods were presented and perceived in a way that they had never been before, helped to shape a new commodity culture.[29] The nineteenth-century fairs were aimed primarily at professionals, however, and their focus was firmly on trade and production. At the turn of the twentieth century the emphasis began to shift to a broader public, and to the consumer rather than the producer. This was seen in the Paris Exposition of 1900, which marked the transition from exhibitions at which production processes and technologies were presented and explained in a didactic fashion, to events that educated visitors in a much more light-hearted way on the pleasures of new products and the possibilities of the future. With the rise of international associations and forums for specific groups, expositions no longer needed to cater for particular groups of professionals. Instead, they became increasingly geared towards an undifferentiated public. Objects and information began to be presented, not as raw data, but in more entertaining contexts that aimed to arouse in the public the desire to purchase goods and services. While peace and progress remained the catchwords of expositions, profit became the more immediate concern for exhibitors.

To display the world to the world at the dawn of a new century would obviously garner enormous prestige for the host nation. The news that the Germans were thinking about staging an exposition in 1900 filled the French with horror, and they quickly announced that Paris, the queen city of expositions, would host an event in that year.[30] The exhibition occupied a greater portion of the capital than ever before (pl. 11). Entry was through the Porte Monumentale, where visitors were greeted with a magnificent panorama of the exposition (pl. 12). The layout of many different palaces and national pavilions did not immediately suggest an exhibition, more a city within a city. Nor did the exposition have a particularly coherent narrative or strong didactic themes. It was no longer a site in which to compare the products of different nations or to trace the development of particular industries; it was an environment designed for the *flâneur*.[31] The Paris Exposition of 1900 was a place to enjoy while wandering at leisure, or, if you wanted to rest your legs, while being carried around on the *trottoire roulant*, the moving pavement (pl. 13).[32]

The shift in exposition ideology is seen in many of the early twentieth-century events, where an officially stated aim to educate citizens about the merits of technology in order to bring about peace and social harmony was generally overshadowed by the exhibitors' desire to educate the public to be

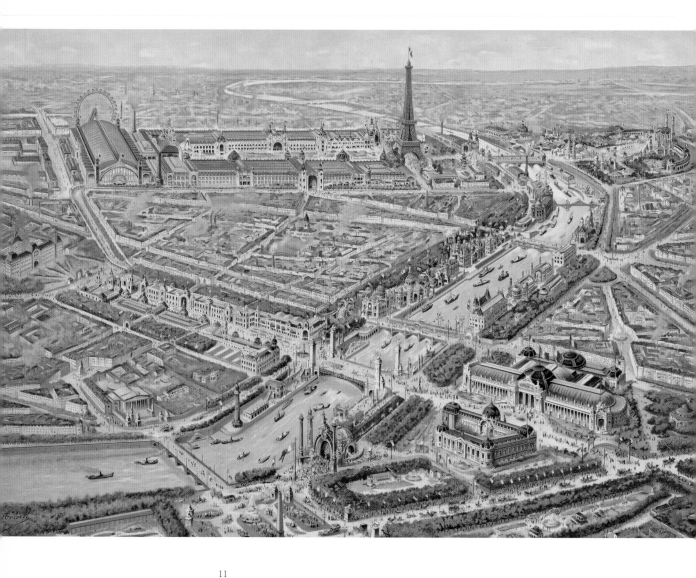

11

Vue générale de l'Exposition Paris 1900, G. Grivell. Colour engraving. 1900.

MUSEE D'ORSAY, PARIS, FONDS EIFFEL. © PHOTO RMN–HERVE LEWANDOWSKI

In the foreground are the Porte Monumentale, the Petit Palais and the Grand Palais,
while across the Pont Alexandre III are the buildings that housed the decorative
arts displays. The main exhibition grounds, dominated by the Eiffel Tower, are in the
background. Industries were displayed in the buildings around the tower, leading up
to the Palais de l'Electricité in front of the agriculture building. Across the river from
the Eiffel Tower are the French colonial displays in front of the Palais de Trocadéro.
Other exposition buildings line the Seine, with the Rue de Nations on the left bank.

12

La Porte monumentale, from
Paris 1900: Exposition universelle:
Champs-Elysées, Invalides,
Champ de Mars, Palais étrangers,
Trocadéro. Paris, 1900.

V&A: NAL 101.D

13

Le Trottoire roulant et le Phare
allemand, from *Le Panorama:*
Exposition universelle, 1900.
Paris, 1900.

V&A: NAL 630.AC.0003

Behind the moving pavement to the
left are the Tour du Monde and the
Eiffel Tower and to the right the
German lighthouse. The white
building on the far right is the
Navigation and Commerce building.

good consumers. This was particularly the case in the United States, where business leaders rather than politicians took the lead in organizing the exhibitions. The fair held in St Louis in 1904, modelled on the Chicago Exposition, was the largest the world had seen, covering 1,272 acres (515 ha) and with a total distance around the fair of approximately 35 miles (pl. 14).[33] It was a major success, the biggest attractions being the displays of automobiles and aeronautics and the demonstrations of wireless technology. However, the fair is probably best remembered today for the popular song 'Meet Me in St Louis' and a novelty introduced by one of the concession holders: the ice-cream cone.[34]

The strong capitalist ethos of the American fairs was overlaid with explicit nationalism generally fused to a particular celebration. The fair of 1904 commemorated the Louisiana Purchase,[35] while that staged in San Francisco in 1915 marked the opening of the Panama Canal.[36] The official image of this *Panama Pacific International Exposition*, used on posters and souvenir publications, showed a Herculean figure – representing the American engineers who constructed the canal – forcing apart the Culebra Cut with the buildings of the exposition site gleaming in the background (pl. 15). Such pioneer spirit and determination were evident in much of the fair's imagery and rhetoric and most famously expressed in a pair of sculptures, *The End of the Trail*, by James Earle Fraser, which showed an exhausted Indian slumped

14

Palace of Manufacturers, from *The Greatest of Expositions Completely Illustrated: Official Publication*. St Louis, 1904.

V&A: NAL 210.P.24

In front of the Manufacturers building is the monument commemorating the Louisiana Purchase.

on his horse, and *The Pioneer*, by Solon Borglum, who, riding erect on his steed, represented the onward march of American civilization.[37] The major buildings of the fair were laid out around a series of courts, an innovative and successful design, and in contrast to the stark whiteness of Chicago and St Louis were a blaze of colour. The centrepiece was the Tower of Jewels, which was covered in more than 100,000 faceted, coloured glass pieces backed by mirrors that shimmered in the breeze (pl. 16).

The rising commercialism of the fairs can be seen in the number of company pavilions at San Francisco, particularly those of the railroads. One of the first companies to have a single building within which to exhibit its products was the Singer Sewing Machine Company at Philadelphia in 1876. At 1893 the White Star Steamship Line had a separate building, as did Krupp, the German munitions company. There were also company buildings at Paris in 1889 and 1900, but the trend was most visible, unsurprisingly, in the United States. At the *Century of Progress International Exposition* held in Chicago in 1933–4, buildings such as those of General Motors, Chrysler and Sears, Roebuck and Company were major attractions. This was the first fair devoted

15

ABOVE LEFT: *Panama Pacific International Exposition San Francisco 1915*. Souvenir booklet cover, Perham Nahl. 1915.

THE MITCHELL WOLFSON, JR, COLLECTION, WOLFSONIAN-FLORIDA INTERNATIONAL UNIVERSITY, MIAMI BEACH, FLORIDA

16

ABOVE RIGHT: *Tower of Jewels*, from *The Splendors of the Panama-Pacific International Exposition in Hand Coloured Illustrations*. San Francisco, 1915.

V&A: NAL PC. 7–9

17
View of Northerly Island looking north-east, from *A Century of Progress Exposition Chicago 1933*. Chicago, 1933.
V&A: NAL 604.AC.0040

The large red building in the centre is the Electricity Building, with behind the Social Science Building, the Skytrain and the Hall of States, and in front the Enchanted Island and Horticultural Building. The bright colour scheme of the exposition was created by Joseph Urban, a well-known designer of Broadway stage sets.

specifically to the theme of science, which was presented as the means by which the country would rise out of the Depression and through which American society and culture would progress ever forwards (pl. 17).[38]

Important fairs, such as those held at Liège in 1905 and Brussels in 1910, were also staged in other parts of the world in the early twentieth century. The latter year even saw an international exposition in Nanjing, held to promote China's products and stimulate economic modernization.[39] In 1902 in Turin and in 1925 in Paris exhibitions dedicated to modern decorative arts were staged, while one of the most spectacular international expositions was held in Barcelona in 1929 (pl. 18).[40]

By this time the great proliferation of expositions, the conflict of interests and inevitable confusion between events and participants, and the sometimes poor organization, had led to calls from various governments for some kind of system of control. In Paris in 1928 delegates from 31 countries signed a convention that brought order to world expositions by regulating

18
Night-time view of the entrance to the exposition of 1929 with the Palau Nacional in the background, from *Exposición internacional Barcelona: MCMXXIX*. Barcelona, 1929.
V&A: NAL 49.B.51

19
Poster for the Paris *Exposition
Internationale des Arts et
Techniques dans la Vie Moderne*
of 1937, Leonetto Cappiello.
Colour lithograph. 1937.
V&A: E.286–2006

their frequency and outlining the rights and
obligations of exhibitors and organizers. At the same
time the Bureau International des Expositions (BIE)
was created in order to ensure compliance with the
provisions. Under the convention, which has been
amended a number of times, the BIE recognizes
and supports both major and smaller international
expositions, as well as specialist exhibitions such as
the Milan Triennale.[41]

Under the terms of the convention of 1928, the
*Exposition Internationale des Arts et Techniques
dans la Vie Moderne* of 1937 was rated only
as a second-category exhibition, yet it was one of
the most significant of the interwar years. It was
also the last to be held in Paris. France at this time
was politically divided and crippled by inflation and
soaring unemployment. The exposition was launched
specifically to create jobs and help the economy,
rather than for the benefit of all mankind, something
reflected in the title of the event, which dropped the
loftier *universelle* in favour of art and technologies
that were useful in everyday life (pl. 19). The official
literature still paid homage to the twin faiths of peace
and progress, but this was hardly a period when a
spirit of universal fellowship flourished in Europe.
Despite the optimistic architectural modernism of
the overall site, the most powerful and enduring
image of the 1937 exposition was that created by the
nationalistic confrontation of the Soviet and German
pavilions (pl. 20). On top of the great vertical mass
of the USSR pavilion strode the heroic figures of a
workman and a peasant woman holding a hammer
and stickle. They faced the great tower of the German
pavilion, which was surmounted by an eagle clutching
a swastika in its talons.[42] These pavilions occupied the
middle ground of the great vista that swept down from
the esplanade of the new Palais de Chaillot. It was

here three years later that Adolf Hitler paused briefly to look out on the
French capital he had conquered.

Germany was absent from the last great exposition of the pre-war
period, the *New York World's Fair* of 1939 (pl. 21).[43] Commemorating the
inauguration of George Washington, the theme of the fair was 'Building the
World of Tomorrow'. Despite the fact that the world was on the brink of
catastrophic conflict, the event sought to convey a confident vision of the
future. In contrast to the allegorical imagery of the Paris exposition of 1937,
the poster for the 1939 World's Fair embodied a sense of optimism and enjoy-
ment, with a depiction of a woman waving in front of the iconic structures
of the fair, the Trylon and Perisphere (pl. 22).[44] It was at New York that the
old style of exposition came to its definitive end, as presentations of current
achievements that built on past traditions gave way to new, futuristic themes.
While in the past exposition displays had been based around objects that
required explanation, by 1939, if they were present at all, objects served
merely as illustrations in environments of visualized information.[45]

This emphasis on sensation rather than the absorption of information
was central to post-war expositions, which shifted yet further away from a
pedagogic approach towards a more experiential one that used new media

20
General view of the Paris Exposition
of 1937 looking from the Trocadéro
towards the Eiffel Tower with the
German pavilion on the left and
the Soviet pavilion on the right.
From *Art et Décoration*, vol.LXVI,
Paris, 1937.
V&A: NAL PP.45.A

21
OPPOSITE: Aerial view of the
New York World's Fair of 1939.
EDWARD J. ORTH MEMORIAL ARCHIVES OF THE
NEW YORK WORLD'S FAIR, ARCHIVES CENTER,
NATIONAL MUSEUM OF AMERICAN HISTORY,
SMITHSONIAN INSTITUTION

The Perisphere and Trylon stand at
the centre with, directly in front, the
New York City Building and the large
General Motors and Ford buildings.
Behind are the Washington Statue
and the Central Mall, which leads up
to the Lagoon of Nations and the
Federal Building.

22
LEFT: Poster for the *New York
World's Fair* of 1939, Albert Staehle.
Colour lithograph. 1939.
V&A: E.285–2006

23
Poster for the Brussels *Exposition
Universelle* of 1958, Leo Marfurt.
Colour offset lithograph. 1958.
V&A: E.287–2006

technologies. That is not to say, however, that
the expositions held after the Second World War
presented a uniformly cheerful view of the world,
its achievements and possible prospects, for in the
second half of the twentieth century such utopian
visions became harder to sustain. Cold War ideological
battles were played out at the major expositions in
Brussels (1958), Montreal (1967) and Osaka (1970),
and indeed such events provided the only real
opportunity for the superpowers to confront each
other directly and present their different visions of
the future.[46]

The *Exposition Universelle et Internationale*
held in Brussels in 1958 was part of a strong Belgian
tradition of staging expositions and, like the earlier
events, was intended to promote economic growth and
gain prestige (pl. 23).[47] The exhibition's main focus
was science and the new discoveries that would help
mankind, an optimistic and traditional exposition view
of progress that was maintained despite the shadow
thrown by the possibility of nuclear destruction.
Another post-war tension at Brussels was evident in
the host's impressive colonial displays. One aim of the
exposition was to bolster Belgium's imperial presence
in the Congo, but by this time the validity of colonial policies was being
seriously questioned and the exhibit seemed somewhat anachronistic.[48]

The international exposition held in Montreal in 1967 was the first to be
staged on a multi-island site (pl. 24). The attractive setting, thoughtful layout
and good organization earned the Canadians much praise as they celebrated
the centenary of their confederation. At a time of counter-culture, conflict and
Cold War anxiety, the organizers had no desire to present bombastic displays,
instead looking to the humanist philosophy of Antoine de Saint-Exupéry to
provide the theme of 'Man and his World'. The social elements injected into
the exposition suggested a level of uncertainty about the future and the
consumer values so boldly proclaimed at other fairs.

No such doubts seemed to pervade the *Japan World Exposition* held
in Osaka in 1970. Here peace and progress were again the dominant themes

24
View of the Montreal International
Exposition of 1967, showing the
United States pavilion, in the
foreground, and the Soviet pavilion.
LIBRARY AND ARCHIVES, CANADA

expounded in a speech made by Crown Prince Akihito, echoing the words of
Prince Albert 120 years earlier:

> The twentieth century has been an era of great achievements. These
> remarkable accomplishments, colourfully displayed here under the
> theme of 'Progress and Harmony for Mankind', have impressed me
> with the unlimited possibilities of human wisdom. I believe that the true
> progress of human society can only be achieved where harmony exists
> and . . . sincerely hope that with EXPO '70 as an incentive, peoples of
> the world will deepen their mutual understanding and bring about true
> peace and progress for all.[49]

In staging its first world exposition Japan aimed to present a new and positive
image to both its own citizens and the rest of the world. The joint imperatives
of nationalism and internationalism that had motivated host nations since the
Great Exhibition were skilfully combined by the Japanese, who presented
themselves as a modern, highly developed nation while consciously preserving
their own identity.[50] Realizing that modern means of communication had

25
The Symbol Zone at the Osaka
Exposition of 1970, Kenzo Tange,
with Taro Okamoto's *Tower of the
Sun* rising through the roof.
PHOTOGRAPH COURTESY OF THE TOKYO
SHIMBUN © THE TOKYO SHIMBUN

rendered the didactics of the nineteenth century and the visual explanations
of the pre-war period obsolete, they focused instead on the role of expositions
as important meeting places where people could share experiences and build
a new global consciousness. In the vast Symbol Zone that dominated the Expo
'70 site, the ritual, spiritual and communal elements of traditional Japanese
festivals were united with multi-media, multi-sensory 'total experiences', to
inspire visitors to reach new understandings as a result of spontaneous
realizations rather than rigid displays (pl. 25).[51]

Expositions of the size and significance of Osaka did not take place again

until Lisbon in 1998 and Hanover in 2000. At the latter Germany finally had
the opportunity, denied it by France in 1900, to present an exposition at the
symbolic turning of a century. The focus was ecological, highlighting a major
global concern of the early twenty-first century. This subject was further
developed at the major exposition held at Aichi, Japan, in 2005, which had
'Nature's Wisdom' as its governing theme and which implemented environ-
mental conservation measures during the planning, actual staging and after
the exposition. The Zaragoza exposition in 2008 will explore the specific
subject of water and sustainable development.

Expositions developed as the first global communication network, but
in a time of mass media and information technology their function is less clear.
Yet they can provide an important forum for addressing various issues facing
the world. The growing impact of increased urbanization will be explored in
the Shanghai Expo of 2010, under the theme 'Better City, Better Life' (pl. 26).
Today, international expositions continue to offer a collective, physical
experience capable of instructing and entertaining on an enormous scale. With
70 million visitors expected at Expo 2010, it seems likely that China, 100 years
after it hosted its first exposition and as it assumes a new role on the world
stage, will do so in a more spectacular way than ever before.

26
Impression of the Shanghai
Exposition of 2010: Bird's-eye view
of the Expo site.
BUREAU OF SHANGHAI WORLD EXPO
COORDINATION

THE CITY TRANSFORMED

The architecture of successive international exhibitions is part of the history of modern architecture itself. They have been a laboratory for architectural experiment, a proving ground and a show-window in which ideas, structures, styles and personalities have first been presented to the world.

ARCHITECTURAL REVIEW[1]

The most remarkable exhibit at the Great Exhibition of 1851 was undoubtedly the building itself (pl. 27). The Crystal Palace was one of the architectural marvels of the age and had enormous influence on subsequent exposition buildings and on the structural practices of the period. The stimulus for such creativity was the demanding remit that the building had to fulfil. Not only did it need to be erected in a very short space of time, for minimal cost, but it had to enclose a vast space that included a number of mature elm trees.[2] The Building Committee of the Royal Commission held a design competition, but none of the 245 entrants was deemed suitable, nor was the suggestion of the Committee itself. The seemingly impossible situation was rescued by Joseph Paxton, who had remodelled the Duke of Devonshire's Chatsworth estate. Using the essential elements of the great conservatories he had created for the duke, Paxton designed a giant greenhouse of iron, glass

27
Aeronautic View of the Palace of Industry for All Nations from Kensington Gardens, Charles Burton. Colour lithograph, 1851.
V&A: 19614

and wood. Covering approximately 19 acres (7.7 ha) and enclosing 33 million
cubic feet (933,900 cu. m), Paxton's Crystal Palace consisted of a long
horizontal block with an enormous 108-foot (32.9 m) vaulted transept in the
centre to accommodate the trees. This deceptively simple plan produced an
extraordinary visitor experience, the glass walls and iron ribs that framed the
long vista creating a sense of sparkling infinity (pl. 28). The real innovation of
the building, however, was its modular design. Standardized glass and iron
parts were made in Birmingham and then sent to London, where teams of
workmen bolted, welded and slotted the building together in just 17 weeks.
The Crystal Palace was thus an early example of prefabrication.

The sense of wonder inspired by the sight of this building, seemingly
created by magic, informed the opening lines of William Makepeace
Thackeray's famous *May-Day Ode*:

28
*The Foreign Department Viewed
towards the Transept*, J. McNeven.
Colour lithograph, 1851.
V&A: 19625

But yesterday a naked sod,
The dandies sneered from Rotten Row,
And cantered o'er it to and fro;
        And see 'tis done!
As though 'twere by a wizard's rod
A blazing arch of lucid glass
Leaps like a fountain from the grass
        To meet the sun!
A quiet green but few days since,
With cattle browsing in the shade,
And here are lines of bright arcade
        In order raised!
A palace as for fairy Prince,
A rare pavilion, such as man
Saw never, since mankind began
        And built and glazed!

The international expositions provided a grand stage for architectural advances and an important stimulus for engineering. The buildings, and indeed the design of the overall site, were crucial elements of these events. It was through architecture that the expositions were transformed from mere displays of things into a complete visual and physical experience that both informed and entertained. Some structures survive, but on the whole they were designed to be temporary, and this encouraged innovation and experimentation, making the exhibitions a showcase for new ideas, structures and styles. The expositions also changed the urban environment of the cities that hosted them, and through the organization and infrastructure needed to support them, particularly in terms of public amenities such as transportation, had an enormous influence on the evolution of the modern city.

    The engineering talents that helped create the Crystal Palace and subsequent exhibition buildings were already being used on railway sheds and bridges, but the expositions brought these skills into a fresh arena, revealing exciting new possibilities. The inherent tension between architectural and engineering practice, however, was never far from the surface and often led to uneasy compromises. This was evident in the design for the Palais de l'Industrie built, as a permanent structure, for the Paris *Exposition Universelle* of 1855 (pl. 29). The edifice had an enormous iron and glass

29
Exposition universelle de 1855,
Palais de l'Industrie, vue
perspective, Max Berthelin.
Ink and watercolour. 1854.
MUSÉE D'ORSAY, PARIS.
© PHOTO RMN–MICHELE BELLOT

This artistic impression of the Palais
de l'Industrie corresponds closely
to the finished building. Indeed,
Berthelin's images were considered
so good that they were included in
an album presented to Queen Victoria
when she visited Paris.

vault, far greater in span than the Crystal Palace, with galleries flanking each
side, created by the engineers Alexis Barrault and Georges Bridel. For J.M.V.
Viel, however, the architect in overall charge of the project, this structure
lacked the cultural status of traditional architecture and he clad the whole
building in stone. Despite the criticism this provoked, the sheathing of an iron
and glass structure within a decorative stone casing was copied in London in
1862, became a model for the American fairs (pls 9, 34) and was even used
for the Grand and Petit Palais, the buildings that replaced the much-maligned
Palais de l'Industrie for the Paris Exposition of 1900 (pl. 35).[3]

At the Paris expositions, the pendulum continued to swing between
engineering and architecture. The design for the main building in 1867 was
brilliantly executed by the engineer Jean Baptiste Krantz (pl. 4), while the
Palais de Trocadéro, designed for the 1878 exposition by Gabriel Davioud
and Jules Bourdais, was a stylistically eclectic and flamboyant, but rather
unsuccessful, edifice in brick and stone (pl. 30).[4] The great engineering
achievement of this exposition was the remarkable control and use of water.

Four enormous hydraulic pumps directed water from the Seine to power the elevators in the Palais de Trocadéro, provide the great fountains in front of the building, feed the ponds in the gardens of the Champ de Mars and flow through the pipes under the immense Palais de l'Industrie. The last served to keep the palace cool, making it the first climate-controlled exhibition building. Another innovation was the network of rails under the floor, which made erecting and dismantling the building much easier.

It was the Paris *Exposition Universelle* of 1889 that witnessed the last, but greatest, triumph of French exhibition engineering. The Galerie des Machines, designed by the architect Charles Louis Ferdinand Dutert and the engineer Victor Contamin, occupies an important place in architectural history (pl. 31).[5] The enormous roof, which spanned more than 110 metres,

30

The Palais de Trocadéro at the Paris Exposition of 1878.

BIBLIOTHEQUE HISTORIQUE DE LA VILLE DE PARIS. © ROGER-VIOLLET

was balanced on huge hinged supports, creating a building that was gargantuan in scale but graceful in its overall effect. Exhibited in the Galerie were the huge machines of industry, while overhead a platform running on elevated tracks afforded visitors a spectacular view of these marvels of modern technology and the vast space in which they were housed.

The Galerie des Machines was sadly demolished in 1910, but this was not the fate of the other great structure of 1889. The organizers had decided that the exposition should feature something truly special, a structure that would symbolize French progress and achievement. The competition to build a tower 300 metres in height – taller than anything built before – was won by Gustave Eiffel, but only in the face of enormous protest.[6] Many feared it would collapse, while even more feared that it would remain as an eyesore on

31
Vue d'ensemble de la Galerie des Machines, from *L'Album de l'Exposition 1889*. Paris, 1889.
V&A: NAL 56.D.9

the architectural landscape of the city. A Committee of Three Hundred was formed to voice this opposition:

> Is Paris now to be associated with the grotesque and mercantile imagination of a machine builder, to be defaced and disgraced . . . For twenty years over the city of Paris still vibrant with the genius of so many centuries, we shall see, spreading out like a blot of ink, the shadow of this disgusting column of bolted tin.[7]

Despite the continued hostility, Eiffel built his remarkable tower, using 15,000 wrought-iron sections held together with more than 1,050,000 rivets (pl. 32). It had no real function and housed no exhibits, but the Eiffel Tower became the greatest structural icon of an exposition and today remains the celebrated symbol of Paris.

The organizers of the *World's Columbian Exposition* held in Chicago
in 1893 wanted a tower to rival Eiffel's, but in the end settled for an attraction
designed by George Ferris (pl. 33). This consisted of two giant wheels, each
260 feet (79.2 m) in diameter, clamped together on an axle reputed to be the
heaviest piece of steel ever forged. The wheels supported carriages that could
hold 60 people, enabling more than 2,000 visitors at a time to be hoisted over
the Midway.[8] What they saw as they gazed further out over the main exhibition
site was a White City with grand classical buildings and impressive vistas,
punctuated by monumental sculpture and set around various waterways, the
central focus being a great symmetrical pool, the Court of Honor (pl. 34).

It might have been assumed that the exhibition organizers, led by
Daniel Burnham, would have looked to architects of the progressive Chicago
School to design the buildings of the 1893 exposition, but the chosen style

32
The Eiffel Tower under construction
for the Paris Exposition of 1889.

33

Ferris Wheel and Bird's Eye View of Midway, from *Jackson's Famous Pictures of the World's Fair*. Chicago, 1895.

V&A: NAL 52.D.135

34

Court of Honor Looking West, from *Jackson's Famous Pictures of the World's Fair*. Chicago, 1895.

V&A: NAL 52.D.135

The Court of Honor was dominated by the Statue of the Republic. The Administration Building is straight ahead, with the Agriculture and Machinery buildings on the left and the Manufacturers and Liberal Arts and Electricity buildings on the right.

was Beaux-Arts.[9] With its symbolic links to the democratic republicanism
of classical antiquity, and an appearance that suggested power and permanence, it was viewed as the perfect style to represent the growing status and
ambitions of the United States. The White City certainly looked as if it were
built to last, but in fact the exteriors of the buildings were made of staff, a
hard-drying mixture of plaster, cement and hemp that gave the appearance
of marble. The only deviation from the uniformly classical style of the main
exhibition buildings was found in the intricate ornamentation and bold colours
of Louis Sullivan's Transportation Building.[10] Sullivan was later highly critical
of the prevailing style of the exhibition and the influence it was to have,
declaring: 'thus architecture died in the land of the free and the home of the
brave . . . the damage wrought by the World's Fair will last for half a century
from its date, if not longer'.[11]

Sullivan was correct to think that the *World's Columbian Exposition*
would have a great impact on American architecture and urban planning.
Through its compelling image of harmony and beauty, the White City was
presented as the ideal urban environment. The exposition also showed that
it was possible to organize and order many acres of land, and, through special
police and fire forces, new electric and water supplies, and transportation
systems, control and service thousands of people.[12] As such, it had an important influence on the emerging City Beautiful Movement, which sought to
counteract the perceived moral decay of American cities through a programme
of monumental beautification, which was designed to instil civic virtue in its
citizens. The legacy of Chicago's White City can be found in many cities in the
United States, notably Washington, DC.[13]

The city most transformed by the international expositions, however,
was Paris, which hosted major events on six occasions. By the end of the
nineteenth century the expositions had added a number of prominent features
to the Paris skyline, while that of 1867 had also helped to accelerate Baron
Haussmann's reconstruction of Paris and improve transportation links.[14]
The *Exposition Universelle* of 1900 added more permanent structures, the
Grand and Petit Palais and the Pont Alexandre III, one of the most elaborately
embellished bridges across the Seine and the first to be constructed in a single
span (pl. 35).[15] The need to improve the city's transportation network for the
exposition crowds led to the construction of the Gare d'Orsay and, most
famously, the Paris Métro (pl. 36). On the whole, however, the architectural
features of the 1900 exposition did not attract much praise. Many were built

35
L'Avenue Nicholas II, from *Le Panorama: Exposition universelle, 1900*. Paris, 1900.

V&A: NAL 630.AC.0003

This view from the Pont Alexandre III shows the Grand Palais on the left and the Petit Palais on the right. It is possible the photographer employed a montage technique to give the impression of the different peoples to be found at the exposition.

in a Beaux-Arts style, while others such as the Château d'Eau and the Porte Monumentale displayed a curious eclecticism (pl. 12).[16] European architecture was rapidly evolving during this period and with this came the search for a new formal language. Among the overwhelming traditional and occasional exotic styles, Art Nouveau was a small but powerful presence at Paris 1900, as seen in Hector Guimard's Métro station entrances and in the Pavillon Bleu, a popular restaurant by the Pont d'Iéna designed by Gustave Serrurier-Bovy (pls 36, 37).[17]

The most interesting collection of buildings at Paris 1900 was to be found in the Rue de Nations (pl. 38). Here, alongside the Seine, was a series of houses, pavilions and palaces constructed by the major world powers. The resulting medley of styles was a flamboyant mix of towers, turrets, pinnacles and domes. This was more than mere architectural entertainment, however, for through these buildings countries projected their national characteristics. The United States vaunted its republican classicism, and Germany and Belgium their medieval heritage, while Finland created its own version of Art Nouveau in one of the most interesting pavilions of the exposition. The

36
Métro station entrance, Palais Royal,
Hector Guimard. *c*.1900.
© ROGER-VIOLLET

37
Pavillon Bleu restaurant,
Gustave Serrurier-Bovy,
Paris Exposition of 1900.
© ROGER-VIOLLET

38
Rue de Nations, from *Paris 1900: Exposition universelle: Champs-Elysées, Invalides, Champ de Mars, Palais Etrangers, Trocadéro*. Paris, 1900.

V&A: NAL 101.D

This view shows, from left to right, the buildings of Turkey, the United States, Austria, Bosnia-Herzegovina, Hungary, Great Britain, Belgium, Norway, Germany and Monaco.

construction of such buildings was an important means by which countries promoted their status and national identity. This was a particularly useful tool for those newly emerging on the world's stage. Japan, for example, used its long and rich architectural traditions to help counter Western perceptions of Asian inferiority.[18] It not only constructed specific pavilions, but also displayed models of traditional architecture at various expositions; while at Chicago in 1893 it built a structure based on the eleventh-century Hōō-dō (Phoenix Hall) at the Byōdō-in in Uji.

At international expositions national styles were also on display in specially created villages aimed primarily at encouraging tourism. At the Barcelona Exposition of 1929 a Spanish Village, complete with inhabitants producing local crafts, was created to show the vernacular style of the various regions of Spain (pl. 39). The village was extremely popular and can still be visited today, a unique survivor in the history of expositions. Much of the

39
View of the Spanish Village from
*Exposición internacional
Barcelona: MCMXXIX*. Barcelona,
1929.
V&A: NAL 49.B.51

40
The German pavilion at the
Barcelona Exposition of 1929,
Mies van der Rohe.
ULLSTEIN-BILD

41

TOP LEFT: View of the Trocadéro, from *Exposition 1937: Pavillons français*. Paris, 1937.

V&A: NAL 32.G.71

This view, taken from the Eiffel Tower, shows the two sweeping wings of the new Palais de Chaillot with, in the centre, the Pavillon de la Paix. In the foreground are the Soviet and German pavilions.

42

LEFT: Musée des Arts Modernes, from *Exposition 1937: Pavillons français*. Paris, 1937.

V&A: NAL 32.G.71

43

ABOVE: Pavillon Saint-Gobain, from *Exposition 1937: Pavillons français*. Paris, 1937.

V&A: NAL 32.G.71

imposing architecture of 1929, including the two towers that marked the entrance and the grand Palau Nacional, is also preserved, but the Barcelona Exposition is best remembered for a much smaller building, the German pavilion designed by Ludwig Mies van der Rohe (pl. 40). Present at an exposition for the first time since the First World War, the Germans deliberately chose a progressive architect to demonstrate the democratic ideals of the Weimar republic. The clarity and elegance of the open plan, the onyx walls, reflecting pools and eponymous chairs guaranteed the Barcelona pavilion's status as one of the iconic structures of what was to become known as the International Style.[19]

This new style was in evidence at the Paris Exposition of 1937, although in the official structures the organizers rejected a more radical modernism in favour of one that included a more traditional Neo-classicist element. This was seen in the Palais de Chaillot, which replaced the old Trocadéro, and the

44
Interior of the Finnish pavilion at the *New York World's Fair* of 1939, Alvar Aalto.
EINO MAKINEN, ALVAR AALTO MUSEUM

45
Travel and Transportation Building,
from *A Century of Progress
Exposition Chicago 1933*.
Chicago, 1933.
V&A: NAL 604.AC.0040

Musée des Arts Modernes (pls 41, 42).[20] Other structures in the exposition,
such as the Pavillon de l'Aluminium, revealed a bold new use of materials.
Saint-Gobain, who had exhibited at expositions since their inception, built a
pavilion designed by René Coulon that, except for its metal frame, was constructed entirely of glass. It had a façade of curved glass, hollow glass-brick
walls, glass flooring and even glass furniture (pl. 43). A more rigorous
modernist style was apparent in some of the national structures, most notably
in the highly praised Finnish pavilion designed by Alvar Aalto, who used a
traditional material, wood, to create a compelling vision of modern Finland.

Aalto developed the themes of his Paris pavilion at the *New York
World's Fair* of 1939. Finland could not afford to build its own pavilion and
instead rented a standard, rather lofty and narrow, box. Aalto used this
difficult space to advantage, creating a great undulating wall of wood

suspended diagonally and mounted with photographs with displays of the
exhibits below. The interior architecture and displays were fully integrated
and evoked the sense of walking through a forest landscape (pl. 44).

By the 1930s the United States had abandoned classicism, now
associated with fascism rather than democracy, in favour of a streamlined,
mass-appeal modernism that implied progress in the free world.[21] Futuristic
architecture was the hallmark of the *A Century of Progress, International
Exposition* held in Chicago in 1933. Here architects and builders were
encouraged to use new materials and techniques, in keeping with the theme
of the exposition, and as a way of cutting the costs of construction at a time of
financial hardship. One of the most distinctive structures was the Travel and
Transportation Building, which featured a domed roof suspended 125 feet
(38.1 m) high by cables attached to 12 exterior towers (pl. 45). The Chicago
Exposition also featured modern architecture on a smaller scale in a series of
model homes that were designed to show the latest in domestic architecture,
new materials and labour-saving devices (pl. 46). Most homes were designed
to be durable, convenient and inexpensive – as well as modern and attractive –
but one, the *House of Tomorrow*, was more radical, revealing a scientific
home of the future.[22]

'Building the World of Tomorrow' was the theme of the *New York
World's Fair* of 1939. The layout of the public spaces and the modern
buildings, with their lack of surface ornamentation, flat surfaces and
windowless walls, helped visitors to imagine themselves in a city of the future

46
Exterior and interior views of *The
House of Tomorrow*, from *A Century
of Progress Exposition Chicago
1933*. Chicago, 1933.
V&A: NAL 604.AC.0040

47
View of *Democracity* at the *New York World's Fair* of 1939.

(pl. 21). At the centre of the site were Wallace K. Harrison and J. André Foulihoux's Trylon and Perisphere. The former was a three-sided obelisk, 700 feet (213.4 m) high, which, as a modernized version of the Washington Monument, represented republicanism, and the latter a sphere, 200 feet (60.7 m) in diameter, which symbolized the new social order of the future. The two geometric structures were linked by a 900-foot (275.3 m) ramp called the Helicline, which offered panoramic views of the fair. Inside the Perisphere visitors ascended on an escalator to two revolving balconies and from there looked down on *Democracity*, a vast model of the metropolis of the future designed by Henry Dreyfuss (pl. 47).[23]

The transformation of the urban environment was also a major focus of expositions staged after the Second World War, although some of the idealistic

utopianism of the pre-war period had been lost. The theme of the Brussels
Exposition of 1958 was 'Building the World on a Human Scale', although the
structure that formed the focal point of the site was built on a gigantic scale.
The 335-foot-high (102.1 m) Atomium, designed by the engineer André
Waterkeyn, represented a molecule magnified 150 billion times (pl. 48).[24]
One of the most striking buildings at Brussels was the pavilion designed by
Le Corbusier for the Philips electronic company (pl. 49).[25] This dynamic
'hyperbolic paraboloid' building was shaped like a three-pronged tent and
constructed with a series of cables, over which a skin of individually moulded
concrete panels was laid. The most important feature was on the inside,
however. Here there were no exhibits, visitors instead experiencing an
'electronic poem' of light, image and sound, the latter by the composer
Edgard Varèse.[26]

The architectural show-stopper of the Montreal Exposition of 1967 was
undoubtedly the American pavilion designed by Richard Buckminster Fuller

48
View of the Atomium at the
Brussels Exposition of 1958, from
a Viewmaster souvenir disk.
PRIVATE COLLECTION

49

The Philips pavilion at the Brussels
Exposition of 1958, Le Corbusier.

PHILIPS COMPANY ARCHIVES

50

United States pavilion at the
Montreal Exposition of 1967,
Richard Buckminster Fuller

PRIVATE COLLECTION

51
Habitat 67 at the Montreal Exposition
of 1967, Moshe Safdie.
ROGER-VIOLLET/GETTY IMAGES

(pl. 50). This was not the first geodesic dome the architect had designed,
but it was by far the largest – with a diameter of 80 metres – and the most
celebrated.[27] The structure of the dome was a lattice of interlocking triangles
made from metal tubes and covered by a transparent shell of tinted acrylic
panels. Inside, a series of platforms, connected by stairs and escalators
and supported by concrete columns, provided exhibition space. While the
American pavilion was an exhibition building par excellence, Habitat 67,
designed by Moshe Safdie, was an experiment in better and cheaper urban
housing (pl. 51). The prefabricated concrete units, 354 in all, were asym-
metrically stacked on top of one another in a variety of configurations that
provided 15 different types of dwelling, each with a garden on the roof of the
unit below. Ultimately, the construction did not prove as straightforward and
economical as predicted, but the complex was still a remarkable achievement
and is inhabited to this day. In many ways Habitat was a fitting summation of
the exposition model-housing displays that dated back to the Great Exhibition
of 1851.[28]

Although featuring these and other architectural highlights, the Montreal Exposition of 1967 received particular praise, not for individual buildings, but for its overall layout and the new ways it developed of using and moving within urban space, all of which were viewed as possible prototypes for the future.[29] At the Osaka Exposition of 1970 there was far less overall cohesion, although in some ways the resulting visual contrasts reflected the dynamism of contemporary Japanese cities. The staging of the exposition was, however, part of a massive urban planning policy aimed at developing and improving the host city on a scale unprecedented in exposition history. The central feature of the exposition also suggested new ways of creating spaces within an urban environment. The immense Symbol Zone, by the exposition's chief architect Kenzo Tange, provided a multi-level display, gathering and performing space covered by a vast roof, pierced by Taro Okamoto's *Tower of the Sun* (pl. 25).

Other notable buildings at the *Japan World Exposition* of 1970 were the Canadian pavilion, which was faced with mirror-glass that made it all but disappear; the American pavilion, which was a large pit dug into the ground and covered with a fibreglass canopy held in place by air pressure and steel cables; and the Swiss pavilion, which took the form of an illuminated aluminium tree. The Japanese Metabolists, an architectural group who envisioned the city as an organic structure that grew from modular, flexible

52
Takara Beautilion pavilion at the Osaka Exposition of 1970, Kisho Kurakawa.
V&A: NAL J.N.94

53

The winning design concept for
the British Pavilion at the Shanghai
Exposition 2010.

HEATHERWICK STUDIO, CASSON MANN,
ADAMS KARA TAYLOR AND ATELIER TEN
(HEATHERWICK STUDIO)

The Pavilion of Ideas is an
enclosure that throws out from all
faces a mass of long, radiating cilia,
each ending with a tiny light source,
that sway in the breeze.

and interchangeable parts, formed a major presence at the exposition. Kisho
Kurakawa's Takara Beautilion pavilion consisted of a steel-pipe framework,
into which were inserted cubic capsules covered in stainless steel (pl. 52).
Japan's architects continued to impress at expositions, notably with Tadao
Ando's Japanese pavilion at Seville in 1992 and Shigeru Ban's at Hanover in
2000. At Aichi in 2005, the Japanese pavilion, in keeping with the environ-
mental theme of the exposition, took the form of a bamboo basketwork cocoon
that softened the strong rays of the sun while permitting air to circulate.

The architecture and built environment of the international expositions
have been central to the messages they have sought to deliver, to the experience of their millions of visitors and to their lasting legacy. At a point when a
greater proportion of the world's population than ever before lives in an urban
environment, it is appropriate that the overall theme of the next exposition, to
be held in Shanghai in 2010, is 'Better City, Better Life'. The exposition seeks
to address three crucial questions: what kind of city makes life better? what
kind of life makes a city better? and what kind of urban development makes
the earth a better home for its inhabitants? Not only will the exposition
examine important issues facing the cities of the future, but it will regenerate
and transform a major part of Shanghai itself. It is also sure to provide a stage
for exciting and innovative architecture (pl. 53).

THE WORLD DISPLAYED

. . . Work is being done on the palace of Aladdin both day and night; hour
after hour it unfolds more of its precious splendour . . . The field of Mars
has been changed into a large table laden with Christmas presents, covered
with all kinds of trinkets from every corner of the world . . . The pounding,
hissing and rattling of machines emanates from the Machine gallery . . .
These sounds mingle with the strange nasal and hoarse singing from
oriental cafés . . . This all occurred, I saw it with my own eyes, during the
world exhibition in Paris, in the year 1867, in our peculiar times, the era in
which fairy-tales come true.

HANS CHRISTIAN ANDERSEN[1]

An air of make-believe, of a beautiful but ephemeral illusion, has always been central to the experience of the international expositions. The remarkable array of exhibits, national pavilions, reconstructions of faraway places, spectacles and entertainments offered visitors the opportunity to encounter a whole world on display in one place. The expositions created something that was at once real and unreal, a fantasy world that could be tangibly experienced. In this seeming contradiction lies their magical and mesmerizing appeal.

Like all those who came after them, the organizers of the Great Exhibition of 1851 needed to impose order and meaning on the thousands of exhibits and exhibitors.[2] The classification system they devised for the British section of the exhibition served to emphasize and privilege the manufacturing process. The three main sections were raw materials, machinery and manufactures, which were broken down into a further 29 classes.[3] The classification applied only to the British displays in the western half of the building. The overseas participants in the eastern half of the Crystal Palace were able to display their goods as they wished, the resulting foreign 'courts' proving to be among the most popular sections of the exhibition (pls 54, 28).

There was also a fourth classification at the Great Exhibition, fine art, but this section proved disappointing. The visual arts had to demonstrate an element of technological or industrial advance to be admitted; there were no official displays of paintings, and while there was much impressive sculpture on show, it was used primarily to create points of interest within the vast vista rather than treated as an individual category. It was France in 1855 that, seeking to confirm its status as the world's artistic centre, created a vital role for the fine arts in expositions, with more than 5,000 works, half of them French, being exhibited in the Palais des Beaux-Arts. From that time the display of painting and sculpture became an important ingredient in the expositions, never the one that proved most popular, but certainly the one that bestowed the most cultural prestige.[4]

The fine art display of 1855 is remembered for the clash between France's two artistic giants, the Classicist Jean-Auguste Ingres and the Romanticist Eugène Delacroix (pl. 55). The most interesting paintings on display, however, were shown outside the official exhibition. The jury had selected a number of works by the Realist painter Gustave Courbet, but had rejected two of his most monumental canvases.[5] Furious, Courbet set up his own pavilion, but with so much else on display few bothered to pay the admission to see

54
Turkey at the Great Exhibition,
from *Dickinson's Comprehensive
Pictures of the Great Exhibition
of 1851.* Colour lithograph. 1854.
V&A: 110.G.9

55
The display of paintings by Jean-
Auguste Ingres at the Paris
Exposition of 1855.
BIBLIOTHÈQUE NATIONALE DE FRANCE, PARIS

The central, circular, work is *The
Apotheosis of Napoleon I* of 1853.
The painting was destroyed, along
with many others, during the
Commune of 1871.

56

The head of *Liberty Enlightening the World*, Frédéric-Auguste Bartholdi, on display at the Paris Exposition of 1878.

© ROGER-VIOLLET

paintings that were soon to change the history of European art. Although he made a heavy loss, Courbet established something of a precedent and in 1867 Edouard Manet displayed his works in his own gallery rather than at the official exposition.[6] While avant-garde artists might be expected to take a stand against the establishment, it is remarkable that at events that extolled the principal of progress the latest artistic developments were not to be seen. At the Paris Exposition of 1878 the Impressionists were completely excluded by the conservative Ecole des Beaux-Arts, which controlled the fine art displays. Nor were they, or the emerging Post-Impressionists, to be found at the exposition of 1889.[7]

Up to this point the expositions had presented only the work of living artists, but from 1889 painting and sculpture were divided into *Decannale* and *Centennale* displays, covering the last 10 and 100 years respectively. The latter often proved the most exciting, especially in Paris in 1900, when the selection was made by the progressive critic Roger Marx. Here the artists of the avant-garde finally earned their place at an exposition, if only in a retrospective.[8] The other great highlight of 1900 was the exhibition of work by the sculptor Auguste Rodin. An artistic rebel, who had been accused at previous expositions of using life casts, Rodin was by 1900 recognized as one of the masters of French art, but he still chose to show his work in his own pavilion, outside the main exposition grounds.

Rodin had first hoped to attract admiration at the Paris Exposition of 1878, but that year the laurels were awarded to Marius Jean Antonin Mercié's *Gloria Victis*. This shows a winged woman – the spirit of France – bearing the body of a fallen warrior who raises his arm in one last valiant gesture, a fitting symbolic monument to the defeated yet heroic France.[9] Sculpture had a strong presence at the exposition of 1878, not just in the fine art displays, but also on the buildings and in the grounds of the exposition. Standing at the entrance to the Palais de l'Industrie were 22 sculptures representing the major nations of the world,[10] while statues of the continents and gilded figures of a horse, a bull, an elephant and a rhinoceros adorned the upper and lower levels of the Trocadéro fountain (pl. 30).[11] In the gardens of the Champ de Mars was the most remarkable sculptural exhibit of the exposition, a colossal head of a woman (pl. 56). This was part of what was to be the world's most famous statue, *Liberty Enlightening the World*. The sculptor, Frédéric-Auguste Bartholdi, displayed the head, as he had the torch and arm at the Philadelphia Exposition two years earlier, as part of a campaign to raise funds to build and

transport the giant monument to New York. Visitors were able to climb inside
to look out on the exposition site from the 'windows' in Liberty's crown.[12]

    Another thing that marked out the 1878 exposition was the dazzling
quantity of the goods exhibited, particularly in the field of decorative arts.
In a bold reassertion of the quality of French luxury goods, Sèvres displayed a
grand temple to its ceramic arts (pl. 57). Photographic images, such as that of

57
The Sèvres display, from *Exposition
Universelle de 1878*. Paris, 1878.
BIBLIOTHEQUE HISTORIQUE DE LA VILLE DE
PARIS. © ROGER-VIOLLET

58
*Vue d'ensemble del'Exposition
de la Chine*, from *L'Album de
l'Exposition 1878*. Paris, 1878.
V&A: NAL 51.E.18

59

The Chinese and Japanese sections
on the Rue de Nations, from
Exposition universelle de 1878.
Paris, 1878.

BIBLIOTHEQUE HISTORIQUE DE LA VILLE DE
PARIS. © ROGER-VIOLLET

the Chinese display, reveal the great mass of objects that were shown (pl. 58).
This was an important moment for China, for it was the first time that the
country had formally participated in a French exposition.[13] China was also
represented by one of the sculptures on the front of the Palais de l'Industrie
and on the innovative Rue de Nations (pl. 59). Here, in the central courtyard
of the palace, foreign participants were invited to build an entrance way to
their exhibits, resulting in a striking row of façades that served to announce
the national and aesthetic characteristics of each country (pl. 5).[14]

Next to the Chinese façade was that of Japan. The country had staged
its first display at Paris in 1867, just a year before civil unrest led to the over-
throw of the Tokugawa shogunate and the restoration of the Meiji emperor.
Although new on the world stage, the Meiji government was quick to recognize
the importance of the international expositions, which could serve to enhance
the country's international prestige, promote its productions and encourage
trade. They also gave Japan the perfect opportunity to glean the latest information on the technological and industrial achievements of the Western
nations. Beginning with the Vienna Exposition of 1873, Japan took part in
all the expositions, always providing large and immensely popular displays.

The Asian, African and Oceanic displays at the expositions inter-
nationalized visual culture and had a profound impact on Western art.[15] At
the exposition of 1889, for example, the music of Java inspired the composer
Claude Debussy, while the encounter with the peoples of Oceania triggered

60
Dining Room, Eugène Gaillard,
L'Art Nouveau Bing, Paris
Exposition of 1900. From *L'Art
Décoratif*, vol.28, Paris, 1901.
V&A: NAL PP.41.G

Paul Gauguin's voyage to Tahiti. It was probably the Japanese displays that
had the greatest influence on the art, architecture and design of Europe and
America in the late nineteenth century.[16] The use of dynamic lines and stylized
natural forms that featured in much Japanese art shown at the expositions
had a particular impact on the evolution of Art Nouveau, the new style that
triumphed at the Paris Exposition of 1900. The Métro entrances by Hector
Guimard, the Pavillon Bleu restaurant by Gustave Serrurier-Bovy and the
pavilion designed by Henri Sauvage for the dancer Loïe Fuller were all
important Art Nouveau structures (pls 36, 37), while the interior displays of
the Union Centrale des Arts Décoratifs and several of the national pavilions
also featured examples of the style. Most significant was the pavilion constructed by Siegfried Bing, the major dealer and artistic supporter who had given
the style its name, which contained rooms decorated and furnished by leading
Art Nouveau designers (pl. 60).[17]

The international expositions offered unparalleled opportunities to see
exhibits gathered from all corners of the globe. Many of the Asian, African
and Oceanic countries were present at these events as the colonies of Western
powers. Through such displays imperial achievements were proclaimed and
territorial wealth asserted. At the Great Exhibition of 1851, British colonies,
dominions and dependencies were organized into one giant imperial display,
at the heart of which was the Indian Court, which dazzled visitors with exhibits
that evoked the material riches, and revealed the impressive craftsmanship,

of the subcontinent (pl. 61). At Paris in 1855 Britain also mounted a large display, emphasizing the raw materials that supplied and sustained its empire (pl. 62).[18] As the host country that year, France naturally had the biggest colonial display, housed in a separate imperial pavilion. The colonial displays expanded again in 1867 and in 1878, when they were situated on the hill leading up to the Palais de Trocadéro. The French occupied one half of the space, their larger colonies having their own buildings, and other imperial nations the other half. This area was used again in the next two Paris expositions.

61

OPPOSITE: *The India Court at the Great Exhibition*, from *Dickinson's Comprehensive Pictures of the Great Exhibition of 1851.* Colour lithograph. 1854.

V&A: 19536:11

62

BELOW: Raw produce of India on display at the Paris Exposition of 1855, Charles Thurston Thompson.

V&A: 33.377

63

RIGHT: *La Village Canaque à l'Esplanade des Invalides*, from *Livre d'or de l'Exposition*. Paris, 1889.

V&A: NAL A.21.18

By 1889 the imperial display had expanded into a whole town of pavilions and palaces, divided by streets and alleyways named after the different colonies. Walking along L'Avenue de Gabon and Le Passage du Tonkin, visitors were literally transported around the world. What made 1889 different from previous expositions was that people from Africa, Asia and Oceania were present, not just as waiters, craftsmen or shop sellers, but purely as objects of display. Groups of people from the French colonies were brought to Paris, where they lived, night and day, for the duration of the exposition in 'native

64
Postcard of the *Exposition
universelle de 1900:
Les Colonies et le Champ de Mars.*
COLLECTION OF PAUL GREENHALGH

villages' (pl. 63).[19] This shift in the approach to colonial exhibits owed much
to the rise of anthropology and ethnography as scientific disciplines. As
encyclopedic endeavours, the expositions now aimed to show all human life,
to create a total and authentic view of the world. The increasing popularity in
both academic and popular circles of Social Darwinism lent another dimension
to the displays of peoples, their appearance and habits being used to promote
the theory that various races were at different evolutionary stages of development. At the Paris Exposition of 1900, the colonial displays had expanded
still further, becoming one of the most impressive aspects of the whole site
(pl. 64). This gathering of different peoples of the empire in the shadow of
the Eiffel Tower made the power of the colonizer over the colonized explicit
and encouraged French enthusiasm for the policies of empire.[20]

For the majority of visitors, however, such displays appealed less
to the intellect than to the imagination. Within the colourful assemblages of
exotic structures people could enjoy the sights, sounds and smells of the
non-European world. As one observer described it,

> All Parisians, lifelong or temporary, are now possessed of a magical
> carpet. This carpet, a simple ticket of entrance, is the talisman that
> admits them to the country of dreams. Here you are transported,
> according to your caprice, from Cairo to the Americas, from the
> Congo to Cochinchina, from Tunisia to Java, from Annam to Algeria.[21]

As early as 1867, the lavish pavilions set up in the park around the main building added an escapist experience to the event (pl. 65). Visitors could eat at Tunisian and Algerian cafés or shop in an Egyptian bazaar. The popularity of such North African experiences developed over subsequent expositions. A modest Cairo street at the exposition of 1878 turned into a major attraction at the event of 1889 (pl. 66). Here visitors could shop in the craft stores that lined the street, have their hair cut at the barber's, sample the cuisine of numerous restaurants and bars, and even encounter camels. The authentic feel was enhanced by the estimated 1,000 Arab people who worked in the Rue de Caire.[22] This was a place where you could easily saunter for a whole day, and it was particularly popular with men, who would crowd into the small theatres to watch the erotic belly-dancing performances. Such attractions were more commercial enterprises than colonial or educative endeavours.

There were also European villages at the expositions. Swiss, German, Austrian and even English villages were constructed to promote a traditional and appealing vision of their respective countries. These were particularly popular in the United States. At the Chicago Exposition of 1893 you could

65
BELOW LEFT: *Vue générale des constructions orientales*, from *Grand album de l'Exposition universelle, 1867*. Paris, 1867.
V&A: NAL SE.95–0004

66
BELOW: *La Rue de Caire*, from *L'Album de l'Exposition 1889*. Paris, 1889.
V&A: NAL 56.D.9

67
Buffalo Bill's Wild West Show, from
*The Magic City: A Massive Portfolio
of Original Photographic Views of
the Great World's Fair and its
Treasures of Art, including a Vivid
Representation of the Famous
Midway Plaisance.* St Louis, 1894.
V&A: NAL SH.99.0021

explore a Bavarian village, visit an Irish castle or drink in an English Pub, in
addition to taking refreshments in a Japanese teahouse or a Persian coffee
house. At Chicago there were also various 'native villages', modelled on the
ones in Paris in 1899 and featuring Africans, Asians, Arabs, South Sea Islanders
and Alaskans. One of America's leading ethnographers was in charge of these
displays, lending scientific sanction to the notion that American 'progress'
could be measured against the non-white world, which was presented as
childlike and barbaric.[23] Displays such as the Dahomeyan Village, whose
inhabitants were portrayed as savage cannibals, served only to enforce
popular racial attitudes, particularly since America's own black population
was not represented in the White City.[24] Also emphasized was the triumph
of white civilization over Native Americans. They were treated as a race of
primitives, being settled into tepees and obliged to perform ceremonial rituals,
while the Buffalo Bill extravaganza, just outside the exposition ground, empha-

sized their position within American society in the crudest of ways (pl. 67).

The native villages created at Chicago in 1893 were part of the wide range of entertainments available in Midway Plaisance, the one-mile strip of land running perpendicular to the main site. Here you could also watch tigers and elephants, a mock desert battle between Bedouin tribesmen, an erotic dance and an erupting volcano, or ride high up in the Ferris wheel (pl. 33). This fairground attraction set the template for future expositions and for independent amusement parks.[25] In the main sections of the expositions, too, the attention of audiences was captured by displays that increasingly relied on entertainment value rather than educative content.

From the very beginning, exhibitors at the expositions had aimed to make their displays as eye-catching as possible. Some of the most spectacular were those of food. At Chicago in 1893, Los Angeles presented a 32-foot tower of oranges and Santa Barbara a 55-foot obelisk of bottles of olive oil (pl. 68).

68
Santa Barbara's Exhibit of Olive Oil, from *The Magic City: A Massive Portfolio of Original Photographic Views of the Great World's Fair and its Treasures of Art, including a Vivid Representation of the Famous Midway Plaisance*. St Louis, 1894.
V&A: NAL SH.99.0021

69
Panorama de l'Isthme de Suez,
from *Grand album de l'Exposition*
universelle 1867. Paris, 1867.
V&A: NAL SE.95–0004

Such curious edifices were constructed to reveal the natural bounties of these
Californian counties. There were also sculptures made out of chocolate or
butter, sometimes created to market the product or demonstrate the wonders
of refrigeration techniques, but often purely as novelties – the chocolate
Venus de Milo exhibited by the Americans at the exposition of 1889, for
example, rather bemused the Parisian audiences.

Many exposition attractions used the techniques and grand visual
appeal of the panorama.[26] At least seven major panorama were shown at
the exposition of 1889, the most famous being *The History of the Century*,
painted by Alfred Stevens and Henri Gervex, which showed almost a thousand
of the most prominent people of France from the time of the Revolution to
the mid-nineteenth century. Other attractions relied on models rather than
painted surfaces to create the illusion of vast landscapes. One of the first of
these was the immense working model of the Suez Canal shown at the Paris
Exposition of 1867 (pl. 69). Nearly fifty years later, at the San Francisco
Exposition of 1915, visitors were transported around a 5-acre (2 ha) model
of the Panama Canal on a moving platform while listening to a commentary
on telephone handsets.[27]

The embracing and intermingling of high and popular culture greatly increased the variety of experiences available to exposition visitors. At the Paris Exposition of 1900 it was possible, within the space of a day, to view masterpieces of European painting, listen to an orchestra, try out the latest inventions, descend into a mineshaft, walk through 'Old Paris', visit the Swiss alps, travel on the *Trans-Siberian Railway Panorama* from Moscow to Beijing or take a *Tour du Monde*, in which painted scenes of various countries were animated by performances in the foreground by indigenous peoples (pl. 70). The most spectacular panoramic simulation was Hugo d'Alési's *Mareorama*, in which up to 700 people stood on a platform that resembled a ship's deck and that, thanks to hydraulic cylinders and electric motors, pitched and rolled as if on the high seas (pl. 71). Two gigantic canvases, each 750 metres long and 15 metres high, unrolled from port to starboard, revealing some of the most exciting views to be found on a voyage from Marseilles to Yokohama. Special lighting effects added to the authentic feel, as did actors playing the ship's crew and air that was blown through kelp to create the feel and smell of sea breezes.

Many of the entertainments available at expositions involved rides of

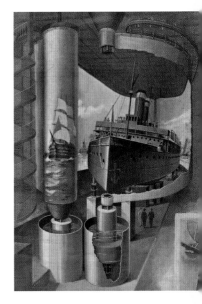

72
La Ballon captif de la Cour de Carousel, from *L'Album de l'Exposition 1878*. Paris, 1878.
V&A: NAL 51.E.18

73
The *Wings of a Century* pageant from *A Century of Progress Exposition Chicago 1933*. Chicago, 1933.
V&A: NAL 604.AC.0040

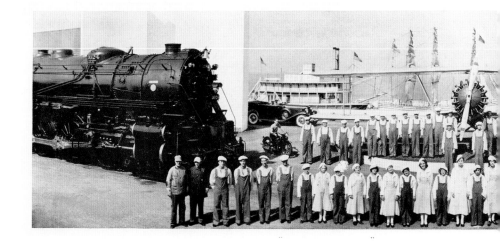

some kind. The earliest of these, the captive balloon rides of the early Paris expositions, gave visitors a breath-taking experience and a magnificent view of the exhibition site (pl. 72). The Ferris wheel that was a feature of expositions from 1893 provided a similar mixture of excitement and spectacle, as did taking the elevators to the top of the Eiffel Tower. Other rides were ones of fantasy, some of the most popular being those that offered a journey into outer space. At the *Pan-American Exposition* in Buffalo in 1901 visitors could go on *A Trip to the Moon,* touring the stars and planets before exploring 'the palace of the Man on the Moon, where all were entertained with a revel of the "Maids of the Moon"'.[28] A trip to Mars formed the epilogue of the elaborate *Wings of a Century* pageant at the Chicago Exposition of 1933. This was enacted on a huge triple stage and told the story of the progress of transportation with carts and wagons, eleven different locomotives, various automobiles, two aeroplanes, numerous bicycles and five boats (pl. 73).

Railroads on Parade was a similar pageant at the *New York World's Fair* in 1939. This exposition featured a wide variety of entertainments, including a parachute jump, *Arctic Girls' Temple of Ice*, the *Congress of Beauty*, Frank Buck's *Jungleland*, a penguin island and the swimming spectacular of Billy Rose's *Aquacade.* An underwater theme was also part of the most remarkable attraction of the amusement zone, Salvador Dalí's *Dream of Venus* pavilion (pl. 74). After buying tickets at a fish-head booth, visitors entered an erotic fantasy where 'mermaids' swam in a large tank full of incongruous objects

74
Façade of the *Dream of Venus* pavilion at the *New York World's Fair* of 1939, Salvador Dalí.

wearing only girdles and fish-net stockings, and a topless 'Venus' slept on a 36-foot (10.9 m) bed of red satin surrounded by various mannequins. Dalí's Surrealist extravaganza stood in marked contrast to the slick, streamlined modernist architecture and interiors that dominated the 1939 exposition site.[29]

A Surrealist experience was provided by the Le Pavillon de l'Elégance at the Paris Exposition of 1937 (pl. 75). The designers Emile Aillaud, Etienne Kohlmann and Max Vibert created a highly theatrical, and somewhat unsettling, space that was made all the more dramatic by Robert Couturier's giant mannequins, roughly modelled in plaster but dressed in the most elegant of French couture fashions.[30] Art and design were prominently featured at this exposition, one of the specific goals of the event being to promote the work of artists and craftsmen who had been badly affected by the world economic crises. A new Musée des Arts Modernes was built (pl. 42), which for the exposition housed a retrospective exhibition of French masterpieces, and there were pavilions devoted to contemporary French crafts, artist decorators and decorative arts. Artists were employed to create large murals. Robert and Sonia Delaunay decorated the Pavillon des Chemins de Fer and the Pavillon de l'Aéronautique (see pl. 92),[31] and Fernand Léger the Palais de la Découverte, while the Palais de la Lumière et l'Electricité contained Raoul Dufy's vast *La Fée Electricité*, one of the few murals to survive (pl. 76).[32]

At the exposition of 1937 the belief in the persuasive power of art was seen most clearly in the Spanish pavilion. To elicit support for the Republic as it battled Franco's fascist forces, Spain chose to display its cultural rather than industrial achievements. The modernist pavilion, designed by J.L. Sert and L. La Casa, contained work by the country's leading artists. Pablo Picasso was asked to provide the centrepiece of the display, in a space 33 feet (10.1 m) long and 11.5 feet (3.5 m) wide. The subject matter for what was to be the artist's largest work to date was provided only a short time before the exposition opened when the Basque town of Guernica was destroyed in a bombing

75
Salle de la Haute Couture in
Le Pavillon de l'Elégance.
From *Art et Décoration*, vol.LXVI,
Paris, 1937.
V&A: NAL PP.45.A

76
La Fée Electricité, Raoul Dufy,
in the Palais de la Lumière et
l'Electricité at the Paris Exposition
of 1937.
© ROGER-VIOLLET

77
Guernica, Pablo Picasso and the
Mercury Fountain, Alexander
Calder, in the Spanish pavilion at
the Paris Exposition of 1937.
© MINISTÈRE DE LA CULTURE /
MÉDIATHÈQUE DU PATRIMOINE, DIST.
RMN / © BARANGER;
© ARS, NY AND DACS, LONDON 2008;
© SUCCESSION PICASSO/DACS 2008

78
OPPOSITE: The interior of the
United States pavilion at the
Montreal Exposition of 1967.
PRIVATE COLLECTION

On the right can be seen part of
the art display, with works by Roy
Lichtenstein, Barnet Newman, Andy
Warhol and Jasper Johns. On the left
is the *Destination Moon* display.

raid by German planes flying on behalf of the Nationalists. *Guernica* is
perhaps the greatest work of art ever created for an exposition, an enduring
and potent artistic statement on the tragedy of war (pl. 77).[33]

Art was also used as an ideological weapon at the Montreal Exposition
of 1967. As part of the Cold War conflict with the Soviet Union, the United
States displayed large-scale Pop Art and Abstract Expressionist works that
symbolized individualism and freedom of expression, the core values promoted
by America to mark the difference between its society and that of the Soviet
bloc (pl. 78).[34] The choice of the maverick genius Buckminster Fuller as
architect for the pavilion further supported America's claims of moral superi-
ority. In its displays, the United States also used spectacle, art, entertainment
and the thrill of space travel to deflect attention from the Vietnam War.

Art and design thus played an important role at Montreal, but one of
the most noticeable features of the exposition was the innovative use of film.
'Expo 67 is celluloid city', wrote *Time* magazine. 'In nearly every pavilion . . .
the viewer is the target of a projector.'[35] Czechoslovakia proved itself particularly pioneering, making its pavilion one of the most popular destinations of
the exposition. *Polyvision* created a panorama on modern life projected
on revolving spheres, while *Diopolyecran* consisted of a 32-foot by 20-foot
(9.6 by 6.1 m) mosaic composed of 112 huge cubes, each with its own
interior slide projector, which showed a collection of ever-changing images
that told the story of the evolution of man (pl. 79). A third cinema experience

was *Kino-automat*, which related a comic tale of the problems faced by
one man, in which the audience was able to chose what he should do in
certain situations.[36]

The creation at post-war expositions of multi-media, multi-sensory
environments reveals the influence of Marshall McLuhan, the Canadian linguist
and cultural theorist who coined the phrase 'the medium is the message'.[37]
Such experiences were certainly a distinctive feature of the Osaka Exposition

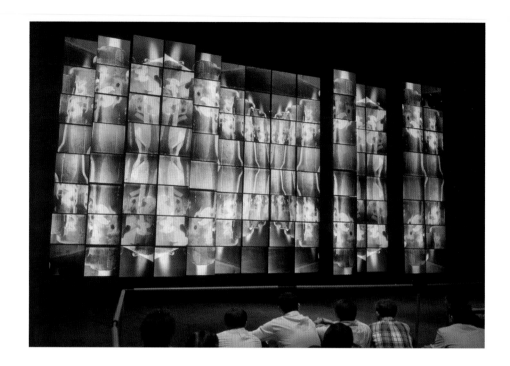

79
Diopolyecran in the Czechoslovakia
pavilion at the Montreal Exposition
of 1967.
TIME & LIFE PICTURES/GETTY IMAGES

of 1970. In the theme centre, visitors were taken on a journey from throbbing light effects and molecular structures, through images that charted evolution from primitive organisms to the emergence of man, a sunlit area of psychedelic colours and a landscape of strange exhibits and juxtaposed images of atom bombs and smiling faces, finally emerging in an area full of futuristic models. Pepsi Cola, eager to tap into the Japanese market, employed Experiments in Art and Technology (EAT), an organization established in 1967 to create collaborations between architects and engineers, to create their pavilion at Osaka. The interior featured an enormous 210-degree spherical mirror of aluminized Mylar that hung above the visitors' heads, while separate sections of the floor created different sounds (pl. 80). Thus visitors to the pavilion both participated in and created the experience itself. For the companies whose large pavilions came to dominate post-war expositions, such imaginative image-building was of paramount importance. So too, however, was mass-marketing, and the fact that there was no product placement at all in the Pepsi Pavilion led to a dispute between the client and EAT.

At recent expositions too, the latest technologies have been employed

80
The interior of the Pepsi Pavilion
at the Osaka Exposition of 1970.
PHOTOGRAPH, FUJIKO NAKAYA. EAT ARCHIVES,
GETTY RESEARCH INSTITUTE. © FUJIKO NAKAYA

to create innovative displays and modern versions of ever popular attractions. At the Aichi Exposition of 2005 visitors could ride a giant Wonder Wheel or, in the Japanese pavilion, enter a 1:1,000,000 scale model of the earth in the world's first 360-degree spherical imaging system. In the Mitsui-Toshiba pavilion, the face of each visitor was scanned and immediately converted into computer graphics, allowing him or her to become a performer in a grand space adventure. At this point one can only speculate on the worlds that will be displayed at the Shanghai Exposition in 2010, although in the vast Expo Museum visitors will be able to explore an art history of world civilizations from ancient Egypt to the present day and take a journey through the history of international expositions themselves.

THE FUTURE REPRESENTED

Expositions are the timekeepers of progress. They record the world's
advancement. They stimulate energy, enterprise, and intellect of the
people and quicken human genius. They go into the home. They broaden
and brighten the day life of the people. They open mighty storehouses of
information to the student. Every exposition, great or small, has helped
this onward step.

PRESIDENT WILLIAM McKINLEY[1]

Conceived as a way of conveying information in a rapidly changing world, international expositions showcased the latest in scientific and technological advances. It was the machine that had given Britain its economic and political supremacy, so it was no surprise that the machinery displays at the Great Exhibition of 1851 constituted the largest group of exhibits and the ones that attracted the most attention from commentators and the general public (pl. 81). The heavy machinery received the longest and most detailed descriptions in the *Official Catalogue*, for, as it stated, they were 'the most direct representation of one of the principal sources of the industrial success and prosperity of Great Britain'.[2] It was the machines – both large and small – that promised new designs, new products, new comforts and conveniences, and new ways of living. And it was through such technologies, it was believed, that progress – not only material, but cultural, social and moral – was to be achieved. The idea that the world was in the process of a structured advance that would lead, inevitably, to a better future for all mankind has been one of the most powerful ideological forces over the last 200 years.[3] Science and technology have been viewed as the primary agents for this utopian transformation and the expositions, through their displays and the stimulus they provided for further advances, were the major stages on which this golden future was represented.

At expositions, the concept of progress always went hand in hand with peace, for it was through the former that the latter, it was understood, would be achieved. Rather ironically, perhaps one of the most notable exhibits in 1851 was the precision revolver displayed by Samuel Colt, while at the Paris Exposition of 1867 it was Krupp's canon that captured popular attention (pl. 82). Such weapons were not viewed as destructive or even threatening, but as exciting examples of technological process and possibly even as deterrents to conflict.[4] In Victor Hugo's utopian vision of the future, they certainly could not stop the advance of civilization: 'These enormous shells, hurled from the gigantic Krupp cannons, will be no more effective in stopping Progress than soap bubbles blown from the mouth of a little child.'[5]

Large-scale machinery continued to enthral exposition visitors. At the Philadelphia Centennial Exhibition of 1876, a giant 700-ton machine, devised by the inventor and manufacturer George Corliss, was the most popular and celebrated attraction. It also literally powered the exhibition. On the opening day, President Ulysses S. Grant and the Emperor of Brazil, Dom Pedro, each turned handles of the mighty twin-cylindered steam engine, setting it in

81
*The British Machinery
Department Class 5 of the
Great Industrial Exhibition
of All Nations,* Charles Burton.
Colour lithograph. 1851.
V&A: 19620

motion (pl. 83). The other exhibits in the machinery hall, connected to the Corliss machine by miles of shafts and belts, then whirred into action. There was no mistaking the dynamic message this projected of the power and potential of the United States.

Various new inventions were on display at the Philadelphia Exposition, one of the most significant being Alexander Graham Bell's telephone, although this was rather overlooked by the public. Notwithstanding this reception, and the awe inspired by the heavy machinery, it was the small-scale technologies most likely to affect everyday lives that proved most popular with visitors. Isaac Merritt Singer had won a prize for the sewing machines he displayed at

82

ABOVE: *Section de la Metallurgie Prussienne, dans la Grande Galerie des Machines*, from *Grand Album de l'Exposition Universelle, 1867*. Paris, 1867.

V&A: NAL SE.95-0004

83

RIGHT: *President Grant and the Emperor of Brazil Starting the Great Corliss Engine in the Machinery Hall*, from *Frank Leslie's Illustrated Historical Register of the United States Centennial Exhibition, 1876*. Philadelphia, 1877.

V&A: NAL 54.C.33

the Paris Exposition of 1855. In 1876 his company, the largest manufacturer of sewing machines in the world, had its own pavilion and employed innovative marketing techniques, which suggested that Singer machines could transform the lives of people all around the globe (pl. 84).[6]

A sewing machine exhibited in 1851, together with the display of Colt arms, rubber products from Goodyear and the McCormick reaper, had revealed to Britain's industrialists the competition they were likely to face from across the Atlantic in the years ahead. At the French expositions, too, American technological enterprise was much admired. In Paris in 1878 it was Thomas Alva Edison who took the exposition by storm, the fact that he was a self-trained engineer with no particular advantages of birth or patronage holding particular appeal for French republicans. At the exposition Edison exhibited his megaphone and phonograph. The latter had been shown at Philadelphia two years earlier, and an improved version of the recording

84

Trade cards produced by Singer
Sewing Machines for the
Philadelphia Exposition of 1876.

JAPAN.

THE Japanese are a progressive race, generally small
of stature, but strong and graceful. They are
patriotic and intelligent; even the lower classes
being less ignorant than corresponding classes in Europe.

The women, who enjoy much more freedom than their
Asiatic sisters, have held an important place in the field
of politics, of art and of letters. Gentleness of voice and
manner, implicit obedience and politeness, are essentially
characteristic of Japanese women.

A girl must, unless she be a nobleman's daughter,
know how to cut and make clothing, wash it, and attend
to all household duties. The picturesque, flowing dress,
which has so long been associated with the Japanese, is
fast disappearing in favor of the tight-fitting Paris
fashions; but the women of the middle and lower classes,
many of whom are engaged in manufactures, still cling
to the older and more comfortable style shown in the
illustration.

Singer agencies are to be found in the principal commercial cities of Japan, and the use of Singer sewing-
machines is constantly increasing.

But One Standard of Quality

There are three distinct types of Singer sewing-machines for
family use, but there is only one standard of quality—

The Best.

There is a wide range of prices, depending on the style of
cabinet work and ornamentation, but whether the price
be the lowest or the highest, the working quality of the
machine is the same and has been fully tested before
leaving the factory.

machine again proved very popular with the Parisian crowds in 1889 (pl. 85).

Perhaps the most famous invention associated with Edison is the electric light bulb.[7] During the period of the exposition in Paris in 1878, electric lighting was installed along the Avenue de l'Opéra and the Place de l'Opéra. When this was switched on it illuminated the streets in a way hitherto unknown, transforming forever the appearance of the night. The seemingly magical power of electricity also changed the look and experience of the expositions, literally providing the public with a brighter view of the future. It was used to dazzling effect at the Paris Exposition of 1889, where thousands of coloured light bulbs adorned the Eiffel Tower, while at its crown a powerful electric beam filled the sky with the colours of the tricolour. Every evening hundreds would gather at the Champs de Mars and on Trocadéro hill to marvel at this brilliant spectacle.[8]

85
Le Phonograph Edison, à la Section Etats-Uni, from *Livre d'or de l'Exposition*. Paris, 1889.
V&A: NAL A.21.18

86
Le Palais de l'Electricité et les
Fontaines lumineuse au Champ
de Mars, from *Le Panorama:*
Exposition universelle, 1900.
Paris, 1900.

V&A: NAL 630.AC.0003

By the time of the Paris Exposition of 1900, electricity was being firmly espoused as the energy source of the future, being cleaner than coal and safer and brighter than gas. It powered everything from the exhibits to the moving walkway (pl. 13), while the banquet held for more than 20,000 provincial French mayors was controlled by telephones at the tables and by electric vehicles that serviced the guests. At night, electricity transformed the exposition site into a fairy-tale landscape. There were evening programmes of illuminated festivities that centred on the Palais de l'Electricité (pl. 86). Here waterfalls and fountains in ever-changing colours sparkled in front of the building, which was lit with 5,000 multicoloured light bulbs and crowned by the Spirit of Electricity riding a chariot, the personification of the magical powers of the new energy. The palace was viewed as

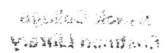

the living, active soul of the Exhibition, providing the whole of this
colossal organism with movement and light . . . A touch of a finger on
a switch and the magic fluid pours forth; everything is immediately
illuminated, everything moves. The 16,000 incandescent lamps and the
300 arc-lamps light up at the same time at the Porte Monumentale, and
the Pont Alexandre III, in the Champs Elysées, at the Invalides, on the
Champ de Mars and the Trocadéro; the Château d'Eau sets its cascades
of fire streaming. Everywhere the soul of the Palace of Electricity
brings light and life.[9]

Paris 1900 marked the shift in exposition ideology from education to sensation
and electricity helped that process, visitors being fascinated by the effects it
could produce rather than how it worked.

From the end of the nineteenth century expositions looked their most
spectacular at night, courtesy of the transforming powers of electricity. The
San Francisco Exhibition of 1915 and the Barcelona Exposition of 1929 were
particularly noted for their night-time illuminations (pl. 18). At the Chicago
Exposition of 1933, artificial lighting provided a major decorative component.
By this time incandescent lighting had become brighter and more highly
concentrated, and tube lighting, using inert gases such as neon, could produce
brilliant colours. The exposition was lit by more than 15,000 incandescent
lamps, more than 3,000 floodlights and numerous searchlights, all provided
by the Westinghouse and General Electric companies. The Electrical Building
also housed a variety of dramatic and informative displays, Westinghouse's
own exhibit having one of the most spectacular lighting effects, which
consisted of illuminated disks of various colours mounted on eight 70-foot
(21 m) towers (see pl. 91).[10]

Westinghouse provided another impressive and popular display at the
New York World's Fair of 1939 (see pl. 94), while Consolidated Edison
showed that electric lighting had not lost its spell-binding effect in the world's
largest diorama, *The City of Light* (pl. 87). In this exhibit, designed by Walter
Dorwin Teague, thousands of electric lights provided a constantly changing
spectacle of New York over 24 hours, the accompanying brochure declaring
that the company was 'proud of the part we have played in helping to build
this first great city of the Age of Electricity . . . [and it] continues to plan and
build in order to provide the best utility service in the world for the greater
city of tomorrow as well as the city it serves today'.[11]

87
Page from the brochure
accompanying the Consolidated
Edison *City of Light* diorama from
the *New York World's Fair* of 1939.

THE MITCHELL WOLFSON, JR, COLLECTION,
WOLFSONIAN-FLORIDA INTERNATIONAL
UNIVERSITY, MIAMI BEACH, FLORIDA

The World's Fair of 1939 looked firmly to the future, but in 1900 too,
at the dawn of a new century, people imagined what the future might bring.
A set of souvenir trade cards sold at the Paris Exposition were entitled *In the
Year 2000* and illustrated a variety of future possibilities, including 'Cinéma-
Phono-Télégraphique', a kind of video-phone (pl. 88).[12] The technologies
that might allow for such developments were much in evidence at the 1900
exposition. Five years after its first public launch, the Lumière brothers
presented their *cinématographe* on an enormous screen in the Salle des
Fêtes of the Palais de l'Electricité,[13] while Clément-Maurice Gratioulet
and Henri Lioret showed the first films in which the image was accompanied
by sound.[14] In his *cinéorama* attraction Raoul Grimoin-Sanson simulated a
hot-air balloon ride, with participants viewing 360-degree aerial film images of
Paris, Brussels, Barcelona and Southampton produced with ten synchronized
projectors. Sadly, this attraction was closed down after only a few days
for fear of fire. Also at the exposition Constantin Perskyi gave a paper at
the International Electricity Congress in which he discussed the latest
electromechanical technologies, coining a new word to describe
developments – 'television'.

New media technologies such as photography, film projection and sound recordings had an enormous impact on the display techniques used at expositions. They also changed how the events were recorded, the Paris Exposition of 1900 seemingly being the first that was captured on film. Images of early expositions generally take the form of engravings or lithographs, although photographs of the Great Exhibition do exist. Indeed, the new art was given a tremendous boost by the 1851 exhibition, which included a significant display of photography, recognized by the international jury as 'the most remarkable discovery of modern times'.[15] The Paris Exposition of 1855 featured the first substantial showing of international photography in France, while the noted British photographers Charles Thurston Thompson and Robert J. Bingham used large wet collodion-on-glass negatives to make a series of remarkable photographs of the buildings and displays (pl. 62).

There is also an extensive photographic record of the London International Exhibition of 1862, stereographic images, which gave visitors a 3-D souvenir of their visit, being particularly popular. By the 1870s photographic images of the international expositions had become more common, since the development of the dry-plate process permitted far greater ease of reproduction. In 1888 George Eastman launched his hand-held Kodak camera, which allowed exposition visitors to take their own photographic record of their experiences. Advances in photography were matched by developments in printing, and by 1900 photo-mechanically reproduced photographs, rather than original prints or photo-reproduced drawings, were the most common ways that the exposition was recorded in newspapers, magazines and official publications. The improvements to photographic and printing methods, together with changing postal regulations, encouraged the development of the picture postcard. The international expositions provided an enormous impetus for the production and sale of postcards (pl. 64). These mass-produced and inexpensive souvenirs provide fascinating documents of the expositions, for they combine official representations of the events with the personal recollections of those who bought, wrote and posted them.[16]

Visitors to Paris in 1900 could not only view the exposition, but were able to look to the stars. Telescopes and other astronomical instruments had

88
Cinéma-Phono-Télégraphique
trade card from the series
In the Year 2000. c. 1900.
COURTESY WWW.TVHISTORY.TV

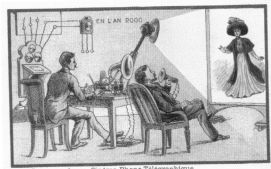

Correspondance Cinéma-Phono-Télégraphique.

89
Poster for the Palais de l'Optique
at the Paris Exposition of 1900,
Georges Paul Leroux.
Colour lithograph. 1900.

V&A: E.423–1939

been shown at the Great Exhibition in 1851, and subsequent expositions introduced the public to the growing field of astronomy through demonstrations and the display of various devices. In 1900 a whole pavilion, the Palais de l'Optique, was devoted to the science (pl. 89). Inside, the world's largest refractor telescope was displayed and visitors could view the colossal images of the moon it allowed (pl. 90). It seemed the future was everywhere in Paris in 1900. The first conveyor belt, new wireless telegraphy, x-ray machines, synthetic fibres, escalators, cars and motorbikes were all displayed.

The latest forms of transportation always drew large crowds at expositions. The Transportation Building at Chicago in 1893 had revealed all the newest marvels, particularly of the railways, with the Pullman Company displaying their luxurious New York and Chicago Express Coaches. There was also a full-size cross-section of a transatlantic liner. By the time of the St Louis Exposition of 1904, it was the motorcar that promised to change the future of transportation, and 160 types were displayed, including steam and electric as well as petrol-driven vehicles. It was Henry Ford who effectively made the

dream of mass motorized transportation a reality and at the San Francisco
Exhibition of 1915 Ford turned out 18 cars a day in a special demonstration
of the mass-production lines of their Detroit factory.

    Exhibition organizers also had to devise ways of moving visitors around
increasingly large exposition sites. At the Chicago Exhibition of 1933 the
Skyride, designed by Joshua d'Esposito, transported people between the two
parts of the waterfront site on 'rocket cars' suspended from a cable 210 feet
(64 m) in the air and stretched 1,850 feet (564 m) between two 628-foot
(191 m) towers. The journey, of just over three minutes, provided spectacular
views of the exhibition, Lake Michigan and the city beyond. By this time the
idea of progress through technology was wholly informing the appearance and
philosophy of expositions. The Chicago event was a celebration of 'A Century
of Progress' and looked, not only to the scientific achievements of the previous

90
*La Grande Lunette du Palais de
L'Optique,* from *Le Panorama:
Exposition universelle, 1900.*
Paris, 1900.
V&A: NAL 630.AC.0003

91
OVERLEAF: Pages from *A Century of
Progress Exposition Chicago 1933,*
showing the displays inside the
Electrical Building. Chicago, 1933.
V&A: NAL 604.AC.0040

"ELECTRICITY AT WORK"—AN OPERATING ROOM

ELECTRIC MURAL, "FOLLOW ELECTRICITY DOWN THE COPPER HIGHWAY"

"ELECTRICITY AT WORK"—POWER DRIVEN STORE DISPLAYS

"ELECTRICITY AT WORK"—PART OF THE 90-FOOT DIORAMA SHOWING ELECTRICITY FROM GENERATION TO USE

Whenever Willie Vocalite, the electric robot, goes into action in the Westinghouse Exhibit he is the center of a fascinated crowd.

WESTINGHOUSE ELECTRIC AND MANUFACTURING COMPANY

92
Interior of the Pavillon de
l'Aéronautique, from *L'Illustration
Exposition Paris 1937*. Paris, 1937.
V&A: NAL PP.10

100 years, but firmly to the future with displays created in a consciously
streamlined modern style (pl. 91). As one of the publications produced to
celebrate and commemorate the exhibition made clear, it

> was planned, by architecture and arrangement as well as by exhibits, to
> throw the minds and the imagination of men forward, into the future . . .
> Forward! Ever Forward! . . . A Century of Progress was meant to be, and
> became, the focus, the concentration, the miniature of the world today
> and the world tomorrow. More than any one thing, determined and
> unquenchable curiosity, the spirit of scientific enquiry, the material and
> the philosophical embodiments of that spirit as they have affected the

conditions of living and influenced the thought of man, have changed the world and set it on its new path of progress. The Exposition, A Century of Progress, was less a presentation of the steps that have led us to it, than a demonstration that here it is.[17]

The Paris Exposition of 1937 was rather different in ambience, with a less adamant emphasis on scientific progress. It expressed the idea that it was through the transforming powers of both art and technology that the world was to progress to a brighter future. This was seen in the commissions for buildings such as the Pavillon de l'Aéronautique, where the latest aeroplanes were displayed in a space designed by leading artists Robert and Sonia Delaunay (pl. 92).

By the time of the *New York World's Fair* of 1939 previously tantalizing images of future possibilities had turned into full-scale, dynamic predictions of the 'World of Tomorrow'. An intense insistence on the benefits of technological progress was seen and experienced throughout the exhibition. The opening of the fair on 30 April saw the launch of commercial television broadcasting with the transmission of the inaugural ceremonies. These included an address from President Franklin Delano Roosevelt, who stated that:

> All who come to this World's Fair . . . will find that the eyes of the United States are fixed on the future. Our wagon is hitched to a star. But it is the star of good will, the star of progress for mankind, a star of greater happiness and less hardship, a star of international goodwill, and, above all, a star of peace.[18]

Only the few hundred people who could afford to buy the new device saw the television transmission, but many more thronged to the Radio Corporation of America building during the fair to see the invention (pl. 93). The image on the tiny screen was seen reflected in a mirror in the lid, while the body of the television was transparent to show that there was no trick to its operation.

Outside the Westinghouse building a Time Capsule was buried that carried, along with an assortment of everyday objects and information, a message for the citizens of 6939. Fair-goers peered into the 'immortal well' for this glimpse of the future, while inside the building they enjoyed one of the major attractions of the exposition, the Westinghouse robot, which was 7 feet (2.1 m) tall (pl. 94). The company had displayed a robot at Chicago in 1933, but *Elektro* was far more advanced and could perform 36 tasks, including

93
Crowds gather to look at the television display in the RCA Building at the *New York World's Fair* of 1939.

EDWARD J. ORTH MEMORIAL ARCHIVES OF THE NEW YORK WORLD'S FAIR, ARCHIVES CENTER, NATIONAL MUSEUM OF AMERICAN HISTORY, SMITHSONIAN INSTITUTION

walking, talking, smoking, distinguishing colours and counting on his figures. He was sometimes accompanied by his electrical dog, *Sparko*.

The major car companies were a dominant presence at the 1939 World's Fair. The exterior of the Ford Motor Company Building featured a mile-high spiral ramp, *The Road of Tomorrow*, on which visitors could test the latest cars, while inside the pavilion the central display was the huge *Ford Cycle of Production* designed by Walter Dorwin Teague. On 16 June, exactly 36 years since Henry Ford had founded the company, the 27-millionth car arrived at the exhibition, having driven across America from the *Golden Gate International Exposition* in San Francisco. Inside the Chrysler Building was the Transportation Zone's focal exhibition, a history of transport, designed by Donald Deskey, which climaxed in a science-fiction-inspired *Rocket Port of the Future*, which suggested how passengers might one day travel from New York to London via the stratosphere (pl. 95).

Popular though these exhibits were, they could not compete with that shown in the General Motors Building. *Futurama*, designed by Norman Bel Geddes, was the largest model ever constructed (pl. 96). Covering more than 35,000 square feet (3,251 sq. m) and extending for a third of a mile on several levels of the building, the model featured more than a million trees, 500,000 buildings and houses, and 50,000 motor vehicles, many in motion. From the comfort of moving chairs visitors could view this imagined world of 1960 and listen to a commentary extolling the virtues of future America, made better by advanced highways and sophisticated cars. Visitors exited into a display of the latest General Motors vehicles and received a lapel badge that proudly stated 'I have seen the future'.

Before the close of the fair war had broken out in Europe and it soon engulfed the world. It was not until 1958 that another large exhibition was staged. By then, utopia might have seemed harder to envisage, but the Brussels Exposition still placed its faith in science to alleviate the world's ills. In a display showing Belgium of the past (1900) and Belgium of the future (2000), it also revealed an image of the future not dissimilar to that predicted in 1939, one catalogue describing the contrast between the 'gingerbread'

94
Elektro responding to the commands of Miss Sue Elias in the Westinghouse Building at the *New York World's Fair* of 1939.

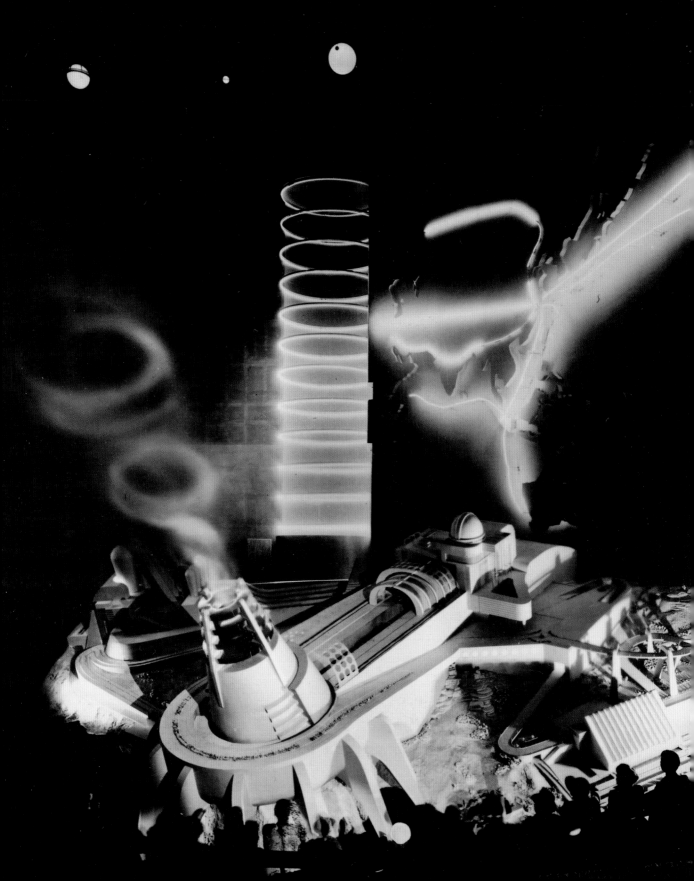

95

OPPOSITE: The *Rocket Port of the Future* in the Chrysler Building at the *New York World's Fair* of 1939.

EDWARD J. ORTH MEMORIAL ARCHIVES OF THE NEW YORK WORLD'S FAIR, ARCHIVES CENTER, NATIONAL MUSEUM OF AMERICAN HISTORY, SMITHSONIAN INSTITUTION

96

Futurama in the General Motors Building at the *New York World's Fair* of 1939.

EDWARD J. ORTH MEMORIAL ARCHIVES OF THE NEW YORK WORLD'S FAIR, ARCHIVES CENTER, NATIONAL MUSEUM OF AMERICAN HISTORY, SMITHSONIAN INSTITUTION

rooftops and painted stucco façades of 'Belgium, past' with the 'free forms and cantilevers of "Belgium 2000". This is Belgium's vision of the Rocket Age. Houses, vehicles, streets and parks are now streamlined, interplanetary travel has become a reality, and thanks to technological miracles there is less work and more leisure for all.'[19]

By 1958, after decades of imagining, space exploration had indeed become a reality. On 4 October of the previous year the USSR had won the race into space with the launch of *Sputnik I*, the world's first artificial satellite. The Soviets celebrated this achievement at the exposition of 1958, where they showed models of Sputnik craft, including *Sputnik II*, which on 3 November 1957 had launched the first living passenger into orbit, Laika the dog (pl. 97). The whole display, dominated by a statue of Lenin, was designed to reveal Soviet successes in the realm of science and technology and to convince the public that the country was about to outstrip the United States in the production of manufactured goods. The Soviet Union also staged a large number of ballet and musical performances, together with exhibitions of Russian art, to counter the West's negative image of the country. While the USSR pavilion

97
The interior of the Soviet pavilion at
the Brussels Exposition of 1958,
from a Viewmaster souvenir disk.
PRIVATE COLLECTION

extolled communist accomplishments, the United States pavilion displayed
American consumer goods and featured hourly fashion shows.[20]

The international expositions continued to be the site of competing
models of modernity, and these were often focused around the space race.
Inside the American pavilion at the Montreal Exposition of 1967 visitors
took the longest elevator ever constructed – 125 feet (40 m) – to the
Destination Moon display. This featured a moon landscape with a full-scale
lunar lander, while above components of the *Freedom Seven Mercury* and
Gemini VII space capsules were suspended, along with models of rockets
and satellites, from enormous multicoloured parachutes attached to the roof
of the geodesic dome (pl. 78). In July 1969 the United States mission to carry
men to the moon was achieved. The conquest of space, and with it victory
over the USSR, was trumpeted at the Osaka Exposition of 1970. The pavilions
of both countries featured displays of space exploration, but only America's
had a real piece of moon rock.

At expositions today it is the possibilities of artificial intelligence,
specifically computerization and robots, that attract the most attention.
The Tsukuba Exposition of 1985 celebrated the latest consumer electronics,

the robots that painted pictures and played musical instruments being the highlight of the event. Twenty years later, at Aichi in 2005, there were robots that collected rubbish, robots that cleaned the floor, robots that provided security and robots that looked after children. During the exposition there was also a special 10-day exhibition that featured various experimental robots. The most popular robotic experience, however, was in the Toyota Group pavilion, which featured an enormous performance in which humans and robots, developed particularly to embody kindness and intelligence, welcomed visitors to a future world and introduced them to 'The Wonders of Living and Moving Freely' and 'The New Relationship between People and Vehicles' (pl. 98).[21]

Since the mid-nineteenth century, technology has represented the whole process of modernization, and nowhere has this been more clearly articulated than at the international expositions. While the idea of a linear progress that draws us inexorably to a better future has been revealed to be something of a fiction, it is still to technology that we look for the changes that will impact on our lives and alter our world. As we approach 2010 it is interesting to speculate about what feats of new technology will take to the world's stage at the Shanghai Exposition and what kind of future city and future world will be envisaged there.

98
The robot performance in the Toyota Group pavilion at the Aichi Exposition of 2005.
GETTY IMAGES

NOTES

Chapter 1 The World's Stage

1   Queen Victoria to Leopold I, King of the Belgians, 3 May 1851;
     see Arthur Christopher Benson and Viscount Esher (eds),
     *The Letters of Queen Victoria: A Selection of Her Majesty's
     Correspondence Between the Years 1837 and 1861*
     (London, 1907), pp.383–4.
2   For further information about the Crystal Palace and subsequent
     buildings mentioned here, see chapter 2, and for more on exhibits
     and displays, see chapters 3 and 4.
3   The profit from the Great Exhibition was used to buy 87 acres of
     land in South Kensington as the site for institutions devoted to
     the encouragement of science and art. These included the South
     Kensington Museum, now the Victoria and Albert Museum,
     which opened in June 1857.
4   The Society for the Encouragement of Arts, Manufactures and
     Commerce was founded in 1754 by William Shipley. More
     commonly known as the Society of Arts, it became the Royal
     Society of Arts in 1847.
5   Quoted in Auerbach (1999), p.23.
6   The 32 countries listed in *The Official Descriptive and
     Illustrated Catalogue of the Great Exhibition*, vol.1 (London,
     1851), are: Arabia, Belgium, Bolivia, Brazil, Buenos Ayres, Central
     America, Chili, China, Denmark, Egypt, Equator, France, Germany
     (comprising Austria; Northern Germany: States of the Stuerverein,
     The Two Meclenbergs, Hanse Towns; Zollverein), Greece, Holland,
     Italy (comprising Naples, Rome, Sardinia, Tuscany), Mexico,
     Monte Video, Morocco, New Granada, Norway and Sweden,
     Persia, Peru, Portugal, Russia, Spain, Switzerland, Tunis, Turkey,
     United States, Venezuela and Western Africa.
7   The mid-1840s had been an economically difficult time, although
     by the end of the decade the recession was easing.
8   See Greenhalgh (1988), pp.16–25.
9   Quoted in Van Wesemael (2001), p.700.
10   See Greenhalgh (2005), pp.109–12.
11   See Bennett (1988).
12   Charles Louis Napoleon Bonaparte, nephew and godson of
     Emperor Napoleon I, had seized power in December 1851.
13   Quoted in Chandler, 'Fanfare for the New Empire' (1986/2000).
14   See Chronology (pp.122–5). There were also specialist events and
     those of a more celebratory and festive nature; see Greenhalgh
     (2001), pp.267–70.
15   *Paris Guide, par les principaux écrivains et artistes de la
     France* (Paris, 1867); quoted in Chandler, 'Empire of Autumn'
     (1986/2000).
16   La Play was particularly influenced by the ideas of Saint-Simon.

See Van Wesemael (2001), pp.224–9.
17   The exposition of 1855 had taken place in the Champs-Elysées,
     but for 1867 and subsequent Paris expositions the Champ de
     Mars, a large military exercise ground, was used.
18   The products of human endeavour were classified into ten
     fundamental divisions. The last of these, 'articles whose special
     purpose is meant to improve the physical and moral conditions
     of the people', was a special category that served to highlight the
     social and paternal aspirations of the Second Empire. Emperor
     Napoleon himself entered a design for workers' houses.
19   The sightseeing boats instigated for the exposition are still in
     operation today.
20   See chapter 3.
21   See William Manchester, *The Arms of Krupp: The Rise and
     Fall of the Industrial Dynasty* (Boston, MA, 2003), pp.129–31.
22   See Chandler, 'Heroism in Defeat' (1986/2000). Often these
     conventions were on a huge scale, such as the Congress of
     World Religions and the World's Congress of Representative
     Women, both held at Chicago in 1893. Also at Chicago the
     Congress of Historians heard a paper by Frederick Jackson
     Turner, 'The Significance of the Frontier in American History',
     which had a profound impact on American historiography.
     The Paris show of 1900 included 127 congresses on themes as
     varied as fisheries, libraries, publishing, dentistry, hypnotism,
     ornithology and electricity (see p.100). The largest was devoted
     to medicine. There were 300 congresses at St Louis in 1904,
     including the *World Congress of Arts and Science*, which
     heard Ernest Rutherford speak on radium, and a staggering
     928 congresses at San Francisco. The staging of such events died
     out in the twentieth century, however, as expositions became
     geared more towards the general public than to professionals,
     who by then had other forums for their meetings and discussions.
23   The architect of the Paris Opéra and a staunch opponent of the
     Eiffel Tower (see p.48).
24   See also chapter 3.
25   See Chronology (pp.122–5) for a full list of expositions.
26   Greenhalgh (1988), pp.127–229.
27   Due to the complexities of planning this enormous exposition,
     it opened one year after the 400th anniversary of Columbus'
     voyage of 1492.
28   Benjamin (1999), pp.7 and 17.
29   See Richards (1990), pp.17–72.
30   The Paris Exposition of 1900 also hosted the second Olympic
     Games to be held in modern times.
31   The term *flâneur* comes from the French verb *flâner*, 'to stroll'.
     Charles Baudelaire characterized the *flâneur* as a 'gentleman

stroller of city streets' who played a crucial role in understanding, participating in and portraying the city.

32 A moving pavement had first been used at the Chicago Exposition of 1893 to transport visitors from the end of the pier to the exposition site, but this was a covered walkway on which people sat rather than stood. The Paris walkway ran for more than two miles and had 'lanes' of different speeds.

33 The third modern Olympic Games were held in conjunction with the St Louis Exposition.

34 The 1904 song 'Meet Me in St Louis' was made famous by the Judy Garland film of 1944 of the same name. The final scenes of the film take place at the St Louis Exposition.

35 Through this purchase of French territory, America acquired approximately 530 million acres, around 23 per cent of the territory of the modern United States.

36 A smaller exposition was also held in San Diego. In contrast to the San Francisco event, the *Panama-California (International) Exposition* featured Spanish Colonial, rather than classical, architecture. It stayed open until 1916 and many of the foreign pavilions from San Francisco were moved there when the latter closed.

37 After the exposition the two sculptures were moved to Mooney Grove Park in Visalia, California. *The End of the Trail* was moved to the National Cowboy and Western Heritage Museum in Oklahoma in 1968, and a bronze version now graces Mooney Park. *The Pioneer,* however, remained in the park, where it was destroyed in an earthquake in 1980.

38 As with other American fairs, that of 1933–4 was celebratory in nature, commemorating the centenary of the founding of Chicago.

39 This was primarily a national fair, most states and regions in China participating, but Britain, Germany, the United States, Japan and Chinese communities in South-East Asia also took part.

40 Because of their limited scope, the events of 1902 and 1925 are not generally recognized as international expositions, although the latter had a major impact on art and design. In 1929 an exposition was held in Seville as well as Barcelona, the former, the *Exposición Ibero-Americana*, exhibiting Spain's colonial wealth, the latter concentrating on industry and Spanish arts.

41 The first *International Exhibition of Decorative Arts* took place in Milan in 1923. It was recognized by the Italian State and was given the title of Triennale in 1929.

42 According to his memoirs, Albert Speer, Hitler's architect-in-chief and designer of the German pavilion, had stumbled across the designs for the Soviet pavilion while looking over the exposition site in Paris and he thus designed a taller building from which the eagle could look down on the Russian figures. See Albert Speers, *Inside the Third Reich* (London, 1970), p.81.

43 In 1939 an exposition was also held in San Francisco, the *Golden Gate International Exposition.*

44 These two posters were not the only official images used for the expositions of 1937 and 1939, but the difference in iconography between the French and American events was marked in all of them.

45 For a detailed description of the displays in 1939, see Van Wesemael (2001), pp.518–39.

46 This subject is explored in *Cold War Modern: Design 1945–75*, a major exhibition held at the V&A in 2008 and in the accompanying book edited by David Crowley and Jane Pavitt.

47 See Chronology (pp.122–5).

48 Two years after the Exposition the African country began its fight for independence.

49 Quoted on the website: www.expo2000.de (accessed October 2007).

50 This striving for a balance between global and local, modern and traditional, has been a mark of Japanese culture since Japan opened its ports to Western powers in the 1850s.

51 See Van Wesemael (2001), pp.573–5.

Chapter 2 The City Transformed

1 *Architectural Review* (August 1967), vol.CXLII, p.87.

2 There were various objections to the felling of the large elm trees that stood on the exhibition site, so Paxton built the Crystal Palace over them.

3 At Chicago in 1893 it was not stone that clad the buildings, but staff (see p.51).

4 Krantz was assisted by, among others, the young Gustave Eiffel. The building of 1867 was not designed for permanence, so iron and glass were acceptable. Like the Palais de l'Industrie of 1855, the Palais de Trocadéro was a permanent structure, so traditional materials were deemed more suitable. Although never much liked, it remained intact until the 1930s, when it was demolished to make way for the Palais de Chaillot built for the exhibition of 1937 (see p.57).

5 See Durant (1994).

6 There were more than 700 entries to the competition to design the tower. Eiffel's most serious opposition came from the prominent architect Jules Bourdais, who designed an edifice in traditional materials. See Mathieu (2007).

7 Quoted in Chandler, 'Revolution' (1986/2000). The group, named for each metre of the tower, included leading names in French arts and literature, such as Meissonier, Gérôme, Bouguereau, de Maupassant, Gounod and Garnier, the last the architect of the Paris Opéra and the creator of the *Histoire de l'Habitation* display at the exposition of 1889 (see p.20).

8 Every fairground and amusement park since 1893 has had a Ferris wheel. Ferris himself died in 1896, but the Chicago wheel was reassembled for the St Louis exhibition of 1904.

9 In 1885 William Le Baron Jenney had built the first skyscraper, the Home Insurance Building. Such tall buildings, hung on steel frames with large windows and restrained exterior ornamentation, were the hallmark of the Chicago School. The term Beaux-Arts architecture refers to the the academic classical style taught at the Ecole des Beaux-Arts in Paris. The main buildings at Chicago were designed by different architects, but, with the exception of the Transportation Building, they conformed to uniform cornice heights and other measurements, and all were clad in white staff.

10 The State buildings, situated in the northern part of the exposition, were also exempt from the classical 'rules' of the main buildings.

11 Quoted in Allwood (2001), p.62. Sullivan made this statement in the 1920s, but European comments at the time of the fair were

equally critical, the Belgian engineer Arthur Vierendeel stating that 'we had expected . . . much better from the well-known audacity, initiative, and originality of the Americans. We have been profoundly deceived . . . in a new world they dared no innovations'. Ibid.

12 See Harris (1990), pp.116–18.

13 Daniel Burnham himself was involved in the plans to improve Washington, DC, which led to the creation of the National Mall and the Lincoln Memorial. The City Beautiful Movement also had an impact in Cleveland, Detroit and Denver, as well as in Chicago itself.

14 Georges-Eugène, Baron Haussmann, was hired to modernize Paris by Napoleon III in 1852. Old twisting streets and run-down apartments were replaced with the broad boulevards and public gardens for which Paris is known today. The construction of the exposition site in 1867 enabled Haussmann to get rid of the steep hill of the Trocadéro – using the soil to raise the level of the Champ de Mars – and to construct railway lines along the Seine and around the city.

15 This created what is still one of the great vistas of Paris, the view from the Petit and Grand Palais across the Pont Alexandre III down to the great dome of Les Invalides, built by Louis XIV and the resting place of Napoleon I.

16 Many of the temporary exposition buildings were clad with plaster, as in Chicago. The Grand Palais was a further example of a great feat of engineering being cocooned in heavy stone.

17 Art Nouveau, 'the new art', was the first concerted attempt to create a modern, international style based on decoration. It was characterized by the use of a dynamic, whiplash line and organic forms derived from nature. See also chapter 3.

18 See Coaldrake (2003).

19 The Mies van der Rohe pavilion did not survive the exposition, but its importance in the history of twentieth-century architecture led to its re-creation, on the original site, in the years 1981–6. Its presence, along with many of the exposition buildings and the Spanish Village, make Montjuïc in Barcelona one of the most 'complete' exposition experiences today.

20 The Palais de Chaillot was designed by Jacques Carlu, Louis-Hippolyte Boileau and Léon Azéma, the Musée d'Art Moderne by J.-C. Dondel, A. Aubert, P. Viard and M. Dastugue.

21 The modern architecture seen in American fairs differed from that of Europe; see Greenhalgh (1988), pp.168–71. An exhibition to be curated by the National Buildings Museum in Washington, DC, in 2009, *Designing the World of Tomorrow: America's World's Fairs of the 1930s*, will explore the architecture and design of the expositions held in the United States during the 1930s.

22 See Findling (1994), pp.108–11.

23 For a fuller description, see Van Wesemael (2001), p.537.

24 Atomium stood on three legs and had nine spheres and contained a restaurant and a bar. Recently renovated, it remains the symbol of modern Brussels.

25 This was not the first time that Le Corbusier had built a pavilion at an exposition. In 1925 he designed the Pavillon de l'Esprit Nouveau, saving a tree on the site in the spirit of Joseph Paxton, and in 1937 the Pavillon des Temps Nouveaux, which, in the tradition of Courbet and Manet (see chapter 3), was outside the

main exposition site. The pavilion at Brussels was mostly the work of Iannis Xenakis, one of Le Corbusier's most trusted assistants, who also composed some of the music.

26 See Marc Treib, *Space Calculated in Seconds: The Philips Pavilion* (Princeton, 1996).

27 The main feature of such domes is that they distribute tension and stress economically by channelling them in different directions. Geodesic domes are solid, yet lightweight, inexpensive and easy to fabricate.

28 The Great Exhibition had featured a 'Model House for the Working Classes', designed by Henry Roberts and sponsored by Prince Albert. Sections featuring economical housing were seen in many subsequent expositions.

29 See, for example, *Architectural Review* (August 1967), vol.CXLII, pp.151–4.

Chapter 3 The World Displayed

1 Hans Christian Andersen, *The Dryad*; quoted in Van Wesemael (2001), pp.14–15.

2 The way that the classification of exhibits changed over time makes for an interesting study; see Benedict et al. (1983), pp.27–42.

3 The physical arrangement of the exhibits, however, did not mirror the classification, all the heavy machinery being placed on the north side of the Crystal Palace – where the power source was located -- the raw materials on the south, and the centre being given over to the more attractive manufactured goods. See Auerbach (1999), pp.94–5.

4 The annual French Salon was incorporated into the exposition of 1855.

5 The rejected works were *The Artist's Studio* and *Burial at Ornans*, both now in the Musée d'Orsay, Paris.

6 Manet also painted a view of the exposition, *L'Exposition universelle de 1867*, which is now in the Nasjonalgalleriet, Oslo.

7 Paul Gauguin exhibited works at the Café Voponi during the summer months of 1889.

8 In the twentieth century, expositions often staged remarkable exhibitions of art, those held in 1939 in New York and San Francisco containing two of the greatest ever collections of art from the Renaissance onwards. Fine art was thus one of the few areas, along with such evocations as 'Old Paris' in 1900, where an exploration of the past was staged at events that looked to the future.

9 The sculpture, *Glory to the Vanquished* in English, is now in the Petit Palais, Paris.

10 The allegorical sculptures were of the Netherlands, Hungary, Portugal, Austria, Egypt, Spain, Persia, China, South America, Japan, Denmark, Italy, Greece, Sweden, Belgium, Norway, Switzerland, the United States, Russia, Australia, England and British India.

11 These now stand outside the Musée d'Orsay.

12 Finally completed in 1884, the *Statue of Liberty* was shipped to America and installed in New York harbour in 1886, as a monument to democracy and to the friendship between the two republics of France and the United States.

13 China was represented at the Great Exhibition of 1851. Official participation had been requested by the Royal Commission, but was not forthcoming. Rutherford Alcock, the British Consul in Shanghai, sent some Chinese objects, but most things on display were exhibited by the London dealer William Hewett. Dealers provided the displays at subsequent expositions until 1873 in Vienna, when China sent its own display. This was organized by the Chinese Imperial Maritime Customs, an organization set up in 1854 to supervise customs collections and run, from 1863, by Robert Hart, who was to become one of the most powerful westerners in China.

14 Such exhibits culminated in the famous Rue de Nations, which featured complete buildings, at the Paris Exposition of 1900 (see pp.53–4).

15 See Greenhalgh (2005), pp.118–23.

16 For the influence of Japanese art, see, for example, Anna Jackson, 'Orient and Occident', in Greenhalgh (2000), pp.100–13, For the influence of non-Western art at expositions, see Greenhalgh (1988), pp.218–23.

17 See Gabriel P. Weisberg, 'The Parisian Situation: Hector Guimard and the Emergence of Art Nouveau', in Greenhalgh (2000), pp.265–73, and Karine Lacquemant, 'The Bing Art Pavilion at the World's Fair of 1900: "New" Art from Old', in G. Weisberg, E. Becker and E. Possémé (eds), *The Origins of Art Nouveau: The Bing Empire* (exhib. cat., Van Gogh Museum, Amsterdam, 2004), pp.189–221.

18 For the British, empire was often viewed as a commodity, a crucial part of the economic life-blood of the mother country. For other colonial rulers, such imperial possessions, although economically important, were presented more as symbolic markers of their status as world powers. See Greenhalgh (1988), pp.52–81.

19 Most of the villages were part of the French empire, but Belgium funded the Congolese one and the Kampong-Javanese village was a private undertaking. The attitudes and reactions of the peoples displayed in this way are not generally known, but they were not just passive victims. Some complied willingly with the exposition sponsors, while others contested their representation. See Rydell (1987) and Greenhalgh (1988), pp.82–111.

20 Colonial displays continued to be staged at European and American expositions into the twentieth century, the exposition of 1937 in Paris having a particularly large one. Britain and France also staged specific colonial expositions, such as the *Colonial and Indian Exhibition* held in London in 1886 and the *Exposition Coloniale Internationale* held in Paris in 1931.

21 G. Lenôtre, *L'Exposition de Paris 1889* (1889), vol.1, no.19, p.151; quoted in Chandler, 'Revolution' (1986/2000).

22 The Cairo theme was quite vague, enabling most Arab cultures to participate in what was a thriving commercial enterprise.

23 Frederic Ward Putnam was in charge of the exposition's anthropology displays, as well as the amusements at Midway. For a fuller description and analysis of these displays, see Rydell (1987), pp.38–71.

24 Appeals for a separate Negro Building had gone unheeded. The only concession to America's black population was the 'Coloured Peoples' Day' on 25 August.

25 The birth of the modern amusement park came in 1875 with the opening of Coney Island in New York, which was influenced by the Chicago fairground attraction.

26 A panorama is a continuous circular representation hung on the walls of a rotunda and ideally appearing so close to life as to be confused with reality. See Comment (1999).

27 The sound was relayed by Edison phonographs (see p.94). Similar techniques were used in *Futurama* and *Democracity* at the World's Fair of 1939 (see p.108). Such displays were the forerunners of the audio-visual presentations that became such a feature of post-war expositions.

28 Quoted in Brodherson (2001), p.48.

29 See Fanés (1999).

30 See Ghislaine Wood, *The Surreal Body: Fetish and Fashion* (London, 2007), pp.18–25.

31 The latter building was also known as the Palais de L'Air.

32 Dufy's mural is now in the Musée d'Arte Moderne de la Ville de Paris. Murals were features of other expositions, notably in the United States. In the 1930s such large-scale public works were part of the New Deal programme initiated by President Roosevelt to combat the Depression.

33 The Civil War in Spain ended in victory for the rebels and the founding of a dictatorship led by the Nationalist general Francisco Franco. At Picasso's insistence, *Guernica* did not return to Spain until democracy was restored. It was housed in the Museum of Modern Art in New York until 1981, when it was returned to Madrid. It is now in the Museo Nacional Centro de Arte Reina Sofia.

34 For the use of Abstract Expressionism as an instrument of the Cold War, see Serge Guilbaut, *How New York Stole the Idea of Modern Art: Abstract Expressionism, Freedom and the Cold War*, translated by Arthur Goldhammer (Chicago and London, 1983).

35 'Magic in Montreal: The Films of Expo', *Time* (7 July 1967).

36 The audience invariably chose the immoral or illegal option.

37 McLuhan sought to explain the effects of media technology on popular culture and human relationships. For his influence on expositions, see Van Wesemael (2001), p.573.

Chapter 4 The Future Represented

1 United States President William McKinley, *New York Times* (6 September 1901); quoted in Rydell (1987), p.4. Tragically, President McKinley was assassinated on a visit to the *Pan-American Exposition* in Buffalo in September 1901.

2 *The Official Descriptive and Illustrated Catalogue of the Great Exhibition*, p.209; quoted in Auerbach (1999), p.104.

3 See Greenhalgh (2005), pp.104–39.

4 At the Paris Exposition of 1900 the Schneider Manufactory armament pavilion had a prominent position on the Seine. It was shaped like a gun turret and had a bright red façade.

5 *Paris Guide, par les principaux écrivains et artistes de la France* (Paris, 1867); quoted in Chandler, 'Empire of Autumn' (1986/2000).

6 Singer did not invent the sewing machine; that achievement belongs to Elias Howe. His machines were also on display at 1876, and there was a statue to him in the grounds.

7 Strictly speaking, Edison did not invent the light bulb, but

improved on existing ideas to develop a practical, incandescent, electrical lighting system.

8 On one evening Thomas Edison joined Gustave Eiffel in the latter's studio on top of the tower.

9 Hachette's *1900 Almanach*, quoted in Allwood (2001), p.76.

10 See Findling (1994), pp.87–9.

11 Consolidated Edison, *The City of Light* (New York, 1939). The Consolidated Gas Company was formed in 1884, by which time Thomas Edison's Edison Electric Illuminating Company was already supplying electricity to parts of Lower Manhattan. Edison's company became part of Consolidated Gas in the early twentieth century and the firm changed its name to the Consolidated Edison Company of New York in 1936. ConEd, as it is commonly known, remains one of America's leading energy companies.

12 Approximately 50 cards in this series have been identified. These include images of listening to the news by radio, flying buses and heating the home with radium.

13 August and Louis Lumière patented the *cinématographe*, a combination film camera and projector, in early 1895. They held their first public screening later that year in a Paris café. One film, *The Arrival of a Train*, reputedly caused a stampede because the audience believed that the locomotive was really coming towards them. This event is generally considered to mark the birth of cinema, although developments had also been taking place in the United States. Thomas Edison had displayed the kinetoscope, a single-viewer peep-show device in which film was moved past a light, at the Chicago exhibition of 1893. That year Edison also built the first film studio, his film *Fred Ott's Sneeze* being the first film ever copyrighted, in 1894. In May 1985 a filmed boxing match was the first movie to be screened before an audience.

14 The films included short scenes of Sarah Bernhardt in *Hamlet*, Coquelin Aîné in *Cyrano de Bergerac* and Little Tich in a music-hall performance. Despite these sound films shown at Paris 1900, however, it was not until 1923 that the first film with synchronized sound was screened in New York.

15 *Reports by the Juries, Vol.II: Exhibition of the Works of Industry of All Nations*; quoted in Mark Haworth Booth, *Photography: An Independent Art. Photographs from the Victoria and Albert Museum 1839–1996* (London, 1997), p.25.

16 See Sweet (2006).

17 *A Century of Progress Exposition Chicago 1933* (Chicago 1933), p.5.

18 Quoted in Zim, Lerner and Rolfes (1988), p.9.

19 *The Brussels World Fair* (Brussels, 1958).

20 See Robert Haddow, *Pavilions of Plenty: Exhibiting American Culture Abroad in the 1950s* (Washington, DC, and London, 1997).

21 Toyota Company News Release, 3 December 2004. This was one of the most popular exhibits at the Aichi Exposition, and people queued for hours to see the performance, just as they had done for *Futurama* in 1939.

SELECT BIBLIOGRAPHY

The literature relating to international expositions is vast. Each event generated official reports, catalogues and guides, as well as popular guides, souvenir publications, commentaries and special editions of journals, many of which have provided sources of information and illustrations used in this publication. This bibliography lists the most useful secondary source material. As well as publications, there is a growing number of websites that relate to exposition history; a selection of these is listed at the end.

Ades, Dawn, et al., *Art and Power: Europe under the Dictators 1930–1945* (London, 1995)

Ageorges, Sylvian, *Sur le traces des expositions universelles Paris 1855–1937* (Paris, 2006)

Allwood, John, *The Great Exhibitions: 150 Years*, revised by Ted Allan and Patrick Reid (London, 2001)

Appelbaum, Stanley, *The New York World's Fair 1939/40 in 155 Photographs by Richard Wurts and Others* (New York, 1977)

Appelbaum, Stanley, *The Chicago World's Fair of 1893: A Photographic Record* (New York, 1980)

Auerbach, Jeffrey A., *The Great Exhibition of 1851: A Nation on Display* (New Haven and London, 1999)

Bacha, Myriam (ed.), *Les Expositions universelles à Paris de 1855 à 1937* (Paris, 2005)

Benedict, Burton, 'International Exhibitions and National Identity', *Anthropology Today* (June 1991), vol.7, no.3, pp.5–9

Benedict, Burton, et al., *The Anthropology of World's Fairs: San Francisco's Panama Pacific International Exposition of 1915* (London and Berkeley, CA, 1983)

Benjamin, Walter, *The Arcades Project*, translated by Howard Eiland and Kevin McLaughlin (Cambridge, MA, and London, 1999)

Bennett, Tony, 'The Exhibitionary Complex', *New Formations* (Spring 1988), no.4, pp.73–102

Bolotin, N., and Laing, C., *The World's Columbian Exposition: The Chicago World's Fair of 1893* (Urbana and Chicago, 2002)

Brodherson, David, 'Eye on the Sky: From Astronomy to Astronautics at World's Fairs and Theme Parks', in John Zukowsky (ed.), *2001: Building for Space Travel* (New York, 2001), pp.45–53

Chandler, Arthur, 'Fanfare for the New Empire: The Paris Exposition Universelle of 1855', *World's Fair* (1986), vol.VI, no.2, expanded and revised in 2000: charon.sfsu.edu/publications/PARISEXPOSITIONS/1855EXPO.html (accessed October 2007)

Chandler, Arthur, 'Empire of Autumn: The Paris Exposition Universelle of 1867', *World's Fair* (1986), vol.VI, no.3, expanded and revised in 2000: charon.sfsu.edu/publications/PARISEXPOSITIONS/18675EXPO.html (accessed October 2007)

Chandler, Arthur, 'Heroism in Defeat: The Paris Exposition Universelle of 1878', *World's Fair* (1986), vol.VI, no.4, expanded and revised in 2000: charon.sfsu.edu/publications/PARISEXPOSITIONS/1878EXPO.html (accessed October 2007)

Chandler, Arthur, 'Revolution: The Paris Exposition Universelle of 1889', *World's Fair* (1986), vol.VII, no.1, expanded and revised in 2000: charon.sfsu.edu/publications/PARISEXPOSITIONS/1889EXPO.html (accessed October 2007)

Chandler, Arthur, 'Culmination: The Paris Exposition Universelle of 1900', *World's Fair* (1987), vol.VII, no.3, expanded and revised in 2000: charon.sfsu.edu/publications/PARISEXPOSITIONS/1900EXPO.html (accessed October 2007)

Chandler, Arthur, 'Confrontation: The Exposition International des Arts et Techniques dans la Vie Moderne, 1937', *World's Fair* (1988), vol.VIII, no.1, expanded and revised in 2000: charon.sfsu.edu/publications/PARISEXPOSITIONS/1937EXPO.html (accessed October 2007)

Coaldrake, William H., 'Japan at Vienna: The Discovery of Meiji Architectural Models from the 1873 Vienna Exhibition', *Archiv für Völkerkunde* (2003), no.53, pp.27–43

Comment, Bernard, *The Panorama* (London, 1999)

Devos, M., and De Kooning, M., *L'Architecture moderne a l'Expo 58* (Antwerp, 2006)

Durant, Stuart, *Palais des machines: Ferdinand Dutert* (London, 1994)

Fanés, Felix, 'Mannequins, Mermaids and the Bottoms of the Sea: Salvador Dalí and the New York World's Fair of 1939', in F. Fanés and M. Aguer, *Salvador Dalí: Dream of Venus* (Barcelona, 1999)

Findling, John E., *Chicago's Great World's Fairs* (Manchester and New York, 1994)

Findling, J.E. and Pelle, K.D., *Historical Dictionary of World's Fairs and Expositions 1851–1988* (New York and London, 1990)

Frampton, Kenneth, *Modern Architecture: A Critical History* (London, 1980)

Friebe, Wolfgang, *Buildings of the World Expos* (Leipzig, 1985)

Gaillard, Marc, *Paris: Les Expositions universelles de 1855 à 1937* (Paris, 2003)

Greenhalgh, Paul, *Ephemeral Vistas: The Expositions Universelles, Great Exhibitions and World's Fairs 1851–1939* (Manchester, 1988)

Greenhalgh, Paul (ed.), *Art Nouveau 1890–1914* (London, 2000)

Greenhalgh, Paul, 'The Art and Industry of Mammon: International Exhibitions, 1851–1901', in John MacKenzie (ed.), *The Victorian Vision: Inventing New Britain* (London, 2001)

Greenhalgh, Paul, *The Modern Ideal: The Rise and Collapse of Idealism in the Visual Arts from the Enlightenment to Postmodernism* (London, 2005)

Harris, Neil, *Cultural Excursions: Marketing Appetites and Cultural Tastes in Modern America* (Chicago and London, 1990)

Harris, Neil, et al., *Grand Illusions: Chicago's World's Fair of 1893* (Chicago, 1993)

Herbert, James D., *Paris 1937: Worlds on Display* (Ithaca, NY, and London, 1988)

Hinsley, Curtis M., 'The World as Marketplace: Commodification of the Exotic at the World's Columbian Exposition, Chicago, 1893', in I. Karp and S.D. Lavine (eds), *Exhibiting Cultures: The Poetics and Politics of Museum Display* (Washington, DC, and London, 1991)

Hoffenberg, Peter H., *An Empire on Display: English, Indian and Australia Exhibitions from the Crystal Palace to the Great War* (Berkeley, Los Angeles and London, 2001)

Julian, Philippe, *The Triumph of Art Nouveau: Paris Exhibition 1900* (London, 1974)

Larson, Erik, *Devil in the White City: Murder, Magic and Madness at the Fair that Changed America* (New York, 2003)

Levin, M.R, and Weisberg, G.P., *When the Eiffel Tower Was New: French Visions of Progress at the Centennial of the Revolution* (South Hadley, MA, 1989)

Los Angeles County Museum of Art, *Japan Goes to the World's Fairs: Japanese Art at the Great Expositions in Europe and the United States 1867–1904* (Los Angeles, 2005)

Luckhurst, Kenneth W., *The Story of Exhibitions* (London, 1951)

MacKenzie, John M., *Propaganda and Empire: The Manipulation of British Public Opinion 1880–1960* (Manchester, 1988)

McKean, John, *Crystal Palace: Joseph Paxton and Charles Fox* (London, 1994)

Mainardi, Partricia, *Art and Politics of the Second Empire: The Universal Expositions of 1855 and 1867* (New Haven and London, 1987)

Mathieu, Caroline, *Les Expositions universelles à Paris: architectures réelles ou utopiques* (Paris, 2007)

Mattie, Erik, *World's Fairs* (New York, 1988)

Meyer, Jonathan, *Great Exhibitions: London, Paris, New York, Philadelphia 1851–1900* (London, 2006)

Mitchell J. Wolfson, Jr, Collection of Decorative and Propaganda Arts, *The Great World's Fairs and Expositions* (Miami, 1986)

Pavitt, J., and Crowley, D. (eds), *Cold War Modern: Design 1945–75* (London, 2008)

Richards, Thomas, *The Commodity Culture of Victorian England: Advertising and Spectacle 1851–1914* (Stanford, CA, 1990)

Rosenblum, Robert, et al., *Remembering the Future: The New York World's Fair from 1939 to 1964* (New York, 1989)

Rydell, Robert W., *All the World's a Fair* (Chicago, 1987)

Rydell, Robert W., *The Books of the Fairs: Materials about World's Fairs 1834–1916, in the Smithsonian Institution Libraries* (Chicago and London, 1992)

Rydell, Robert W., 'Souvenirs of Imperialism: World's Fair Postcards', in C.M. Geary and V.-L. Webb, *Delivering Views: Distant Cultures in Early Postcards* (Washington, DC, 1998)

Rydell, Robert W., Findling, J.E., and Pelle, K.D., *Fair America: World's Fairs in the United States* (Washington, DC, and London, 2000)

Schrenk, Lisa D., *Building a Century of Progress: The Architecture of Chicago's 1933–34 World's Fair* (Minnesota, 2007)

Shanghai Library, *Zhongguo yu shibo lishi jilu 1851–1940*
[China and World Exposition Historical Records, 1851–1940]
(Shanghai, 2002)

Silvermann, Debora L., 'The 1889 Exhibition: The Crisis of Bourgeois
Individualism', *Oppositions: A Journal of Ideas and Criticisms in
Architecture* (Spring 1977), pp.71–91

Sweet, Jonathan, 'International Exhibition Postcards: Tangible
Reflections of the Ephemeral Past', paper delivered at the conference,
Sieze the Day: Exhibitions, Australia and the World, Museum
Victoria, Melbourne, October 2006

Union Centrale des Arts Décoratifs, *Le livre des expositions
universelles 1851–1989* (Paris, 1983)

Van Wesemael, Pieter, *Architecture of Instruction and Delight:
A Socio-historical Analysis of World Exhibitions as a Didactic
Phenomenon* (Rotterdam, 2001)

Wood, Andrew F., *New York's 1939–1940 World's Fair* (Charleston,
SC, 2004)

Zim, L., Lerner, M., and Rolfes, H., *The World of Tomorrow:
The 1939 New York World's Fair* (New York, 1988)

www.bie-paris.org/main/index.php

http://columbus.gl.iit.edu/index.html

www.culture.gouv.fr/documentation/joconde/fr/decouvrir/expositions/expos_univ/expo_univ.htm

www.csufresno.edu/library/subjectresources/specialcollections/worldfairs/

http://expo67.ncf.ca/

www.expo2000.de/expo2000/index.html

www.expo2005.or.jp/en/

www.expo2010china.com/expo/expoenglish/index.html

www.expomuseum.com/

http://expositions.bnf.fr/universelles/index.htm

http://hometown.aol.com/chicfair/index.html

www.historyillustrated.com/texts/expos/

www.lib.umd.edu/digital/worldsfairs/exhibits.jsp

http://pageperso.aol.fr/bottomcircle/Exposition-Universelle.html

www.publichistory.org/reviews/View_Review.asp?DBID=47

www.sil.si.edu/silpublications/worlds-fairs/introduction.htm

http://users.skynet.be/rentfarm/expo58/index.htm

www.westland.net/expo67/

www.wolfsonian.org/collections/c6/index.html

http://xroads.virginia.edu/~MA96/WCE/title.html

CHRONOLOGY

This chronology lists, as fully as possible, the international expositions held around the world since 1851.

Since 1928 the Bureau International des Expositions (BIE) has regulated the frequency of expositions and managed the rights and obligations of exhibitors and organizers (see pp. 31–2). A number of expositions, however, have been staged outside the jurisdiction of the 1928 Convention and these are noted below with an asterisk*. Smaller international expositions and those with a specialist theme, recognized and supported by the BIE, are listed with a dagger†. The BIE also recognizes the Horticultural International Exhibitions approved by the International Association of Horticultural Producers, and the Milan Triennial Exhibition of Decorative Arts and Modern Architecture; these are listed separately at the end of the Chronology.

1851   London (Great Britain): *The Great Exhibition of the Works of Industry of All Nations*

1853   Dublin (Ireland): *Great Industrial Exhibition*

1853–4 New York (USA): *World's Fair of the Works of Industry of All Nations*

1855   Paris (France): *Exposition Universelle des Produits de l'Agriculture, de l'Industrie et des Beaux-Arts de Paris 1855*

1862   London (Great Britain): *London International Exhibition of Industry and Art 1862*

1865   Dublin (Ireland): *International Exhibition of Arts and Manufactures*

1865   Dunedin (New Zealand): *New Zealand International Exhibition*

1866   Melbourne (Australia): *Intercolonial Exhibition*

1867   Paris (France): *Exposition Universelle de Paris 1867*

1871   London (Great Britain): *1st Annual International Exhibition*

1872   London (Great Britain): *2nd Annual International Exhibition*

1873   Moscow (Russia): *Polytechnic Exhibition*

1873   London (Great Britain): *3rd Annual International Exhibition*

1873   Vienna (Austria): *Welt-Ausstellung 1873 in Wien / World Exhibition 1873 in Vienna*

1874   London (Great Britain): *4th Annual International Exhibition*

1875   Santiago (Chile): *Exposición Internacional de 1875*

1876   Philadelphia (USA): *Centennial Exhibition of Arts, Manufactures and Products of the Soil and Mine*

1877   Cape Town (South Africa): *South African International Exhibition*

1878   Paris (France): *Exposition Universelle de Paris 1878*

1879–80 Sydney (Australia): *Sydney International Exhibition*

1880–81 Melbourne (Australia): *International Exhibition of Arts, Manufactures and Agricultural and Industrial Products of All Nations*

1881   Adelaide (Australia): *Adelaide International Exposition*

1882   Christchurch (New Zealand): *New Zealand International Exposition*

1883   Amsterdam (Netherlands): *International Koloniale en Uitvoerhandle Tentoonstelling te Amsterdam / The International Colonial and Export Trade Exhibition*

1883   Boston (USA): *The American Exhibition of the Products, Arts and Manufactures of Foreign Nations*

1883–4 Calcutta (British India): *Calcutta International Exhibition*

1884–5	New Orleans (USA): *World's Industrial and Cotton Centennial Exhibition*
1885	Antwerp (Belgium): *Exposition Universelle d'Anvers*
1886	London (Great Britain): *Colonial and Indian Exhibition*
1886	Edinburgh (Scotland): *Edinburgh International Exhibition*
1887–8	Adelaide (Australia): *Jubilee International Exhibition*
1888	Barcelona (Spain): *Exposición Universal de Barcelona 1888*
1888	Glasgow (Scotland): *Glasgow International Exhibition*
1888	Brussels (Belgium): *Grand Concours International des Sciences et de l'Industrie*
1888–9	Melbourne (Australia): *Centennial International Exhibition*
1889	Paris (France): *Exposition Universelle de Paris 1889*
1889–90	Dunedin (New Zealand): *New Zealand and South Seas Exhibition*
1891	Jamaica: *International Exhibition*
1891–2	Launceston (Australia): *Tasmania International Exhibition*
1892	Kimberley (South Africa): *South Africa and International Exhibition*
1893	Chicago (USA): *World's Columbian Exposition*
1894	San Francisco (USA): *California Midwinter International Exposition*
1894	Antwerp (Belgium): *Exposition Internationale d'Anvers*
1894–5	Hobart (Australia): *Tasmania International Exhibition*
1895	Atlanta (USA): *Atlanta Cotton States and International Exposition*
1897	Guatemala: *Exposición Centro-Americana*
1897	Brisbane (Australia): *Queensland International Exhibition*
1897	Brussels (Belgium): *Exposition Internationale de Bruxelles 1897*
1897	Nashville (USA): *Tennessee Centennial and International Exposition*
1897	Stockholm (Sweden): *General Art and Industrial Exposition of Stockholm*
1898	Omaha (USA): *The Trans-Mississippi and International Exposition*
1900	Paris (France): *Exposition Universelle et Internationale de Paris 1900*
1901	Buffalo (USA): *Pan-American Exposition*
1901	Glasgow (Scotland): *Glasgow International Exhibition*
1901–2	South Carolina (USA): *South Carolina Interstate and West Indian Exposition*
1902	Turin (Italy): *Esposizione Internazionale d'Arte Decorativa Moderna*
1902–3	Tonkin (Hanoi) (Vietnam): *Exposition Française et Internationale*
1904	St Louis (USA): *Louisiana Purchase Exposition*
1905	Liège (Belgium): *Exposition Universelle et Internationale de Liège 1905*
1905	Portland (USA): *The Lewis and Clark Centennial Exhibition*
1906	Milan (Italy): *Esposizione Internazionale del Sempione*
1906–7	Christchurch (New Zealand): *New Zealand International Exhibition of Arts and Industries*
1907	Dublin (Ireland): *Irish International Exhibition*
1907	Hampton Roads (USA): *Jamestown Tercentennial Exhibition*
1908	London (Great Britain): *Franco-British Exhibition*
1909	Seattle (USA): *Alaska-Yukon Pacific Exposition*
1910	Brussels (Belgium): *Exposition Universelle et Internationale de Bruxelles 1910*
1910	London (Great Britain): *Japan-British Exhibition*
1910	Jiangning (Nanjing) (China): *Nanking South Seas Exhibition*
1911	Turin (Italy): *Esposizione Internazionale d'Industria e del Lavoro*
1913	Amsterdam (The Netherlands): Tentoonstelling De Vrouw 1813–1913
1913	Ghent (Belgium): *Exposition Universelle et Internationale de Gand / Wereldtentoonstelling Gent 1913*

1915 San Francisco (USA): *Panama-Pacific International Exposition San Francisco 1915*

1915–16 San Diego (USA): *Panama-California (International) Exposition*

1922–3 Rio de Janeiro (Brazil): *Exposição Internacional do Centenário da Independência do Brasil*

1924–5 Wembley (Great Britain): *British Empire Exhibition*

1924–6 Dunedin (New Zealand): *New Zealand and South Seas*

1925 Paris (France): *Exposition Internationale des Arts Décoratifs et Industriels Modernes*

1926 Philadelphia (USA): *Sesqui-Centennial Exposition*

1928 BIE Diplomatic Convention Governing International Expositions

1929 Barcelona (Spain): *Exposición Internacional de Barcelona**

1930 Seville (Spain): *Exposición Ibero-Americana**

1930 Antwerp (Belgium): *Exposition Internationale, Colonial, Maritime et d'Art Flammand**

1930 Liège (Belgium): *Exposition Internationale de la Grande Industrie, des Sciences et Applications de l'Art Wallon**

1930 Stockholm (Sweden): *Stockholm International Exhibition**

1931 Paris (France): *Exposition Coloniale Internationale**

1933–4 Chicago (USA): *A Century of Progress, International Exposition**

1935 Brussels (Belgium): *Exposition Universelle et Internationale de Bruxelles, 1935*

1935 San Diego (USA): *California Pacific International Exposition**

1936 Stockholm (Sweden): *ILIS (Internationella Luftfartsutstallningen i Stockholm)* †

1936 Cleveland (USA): *Great Lakes Exposition* †

1937 Paris (France): *Exposition Internationale des Arts et Techniques dans la Vie Moderne*

1938 Glasgow (Scotland): *Empire Exhibition, Scotland 1938**

1938 Helsinki (Finland): *Second International Aeronautic Exhibition S.I.L.I.* †

1939 New York (USA): *New York World's Fair 1939–1940*

1939 Liège (Belgium): *Exposition Internationale de la Technique de l'Eau* †

1939 Dresden (Germany): *Deutsche Kolonial Ausstellung*

1939–40 San Francisco (USA): *Golden Gate International Exposition**

1947 Paris (France): *Paris 1947* †

1949 Stockholm (Sweden): *Universal Sport Exhibition (Linguiade)* †

1949 Port-au-Prince (Haiti): *L'Exposition Internationale de Port au Prince 1949*

1949 Lyon (France): *Lyon 1949* †

1951 Lille (France): *International Exhibition of Textiles* †

1953 Jerusalem (Israel): *International Exhibition and Fair Jerusalem Israel Conquest of the Desert* †

1953 Rome (Italy): *Roma 1953 Agricultural Exhibition* †

1954 Naples (Italy): *Mostra d'Oltremare (Campi Flegrei)* †

1955 Turin (Italy): *International Sport Exhibition Turin 1955* †

1955 Helsingborg (Sweden): *H55 Exposition Internationale des Arts Appliqués de l'Habitation et de l'Aménagement Interieure* †

1956 Beit Dagon (Israel): *Exhibition of Citriculture* †

1957 Berlin (Germany): *Interbau (Berlin 57)* †

1958 Brussels (Belgium): *Exposition Universelle et Internationale de Bruxelles / Wereldtentoonstelling Brussel 1958*

1961 Turin (Italy): *International Labour Exhibition* †

1962 Seattle (USA): *Century 21 Exposition* †

1964–5 New York (USA): *New York World's Fair**

1965 Munich (Germany): *International Exhibition of Horticulture Hambourg 1963 / IGA 63* †

1967 Montreal (Canada): *Canadian World Exhibition (Expo '67)*

1968 San Antonio (USA): *Hemisfair 1968 (San Antonio)* †

1970 Osaka (Japan): *Japan World Exposition (Expo '70)*

1971   Budapest (Hungary): *World Exhibition Hunting* †

1974   Spokane (USA): *Expo '74 (World's Fair)* †

1975   Okinawa (Japan): *International Ocean Exposition Okinawa, Japan 1975* †

1981   Plovdiv (Bulgaria): *Exposition Cynegetique Mondiale Bulgarie 1981* †

1982   Knoxville (USA): *1982 Knoxville International Energy Exposition* †

1984   New Orleans (USA): *The 1984 Louisiana World Exposition* †

1985   Tsukuba (Japan): *The International Exposition Tsukuba, Japan 1985 (Tsukuba Expo '85)* †

1985   Plovdiv (Bulgaria): *World Exhibition of Achievement of the Young Inventor Bulgaria 1985* †

1986   Vancouver (Canada): *The 1986 World Exposition on Transportation* †

1988   Brisbane (Australia): *The International Exposition on Leisure in the Age of Technology, Brisbane, Australia, 1988 (World Expo '88)* †

1991   Plovdiv (Bulgaria): *Second World Exhibition of Achievements of the Young Inventors, Bulgaria 1991* †

1992   Genoa (Italy): *International Exhibition Genoa '92 Colombo '92* †

1992   Seville (Spain): *Universal Exhibition Sevilla 92 (Expo '92)*

1993   Taejon (Korea): *The Taejon International Exposition Korea 1993* †

1998   Lisbon (Portugal): *Lisboa Expo '98* †

2000   Hanover (Germany): *Universal Exhibition Hannover 2000*

2005   Aichi (Japan): *International Exhibition of 2005 Aichi*

2008   Zaragoza (Spain): *Expo 2008* †

2010   Shanghai (China): *Expo 2010 Shanghai*

Horticultural International Exhibitions

1960   Rotterdam (Netherlands)

1963   Hamburg (Germany)

1964   Vienna (Austria)

1969   Paris (France)

1972   Amsterdam (Netherlands)

1973   Hamburg (Germany)

1974   Vienna (Austria)

1980   Montreal (Canada)

1982   Amsterdam (Netherlands)

1983   Munich (Germany):

1984   Liverpool (Great Britain)

1990   Osaka (Japan)

1992   The Hague (Netherlands)

1993   Stuttgart (Germany)

1999   Kunming (China)

2002   Haarlemmermeer (Netherlands)

2003   Rostock (Germany)

Milan Triennale

Italia Triennale of Milan International Exhibition of Decorative Arts, Modern Industry and Modern Architecture

1933   5th Triennale

1936   6th Triennale

1940   7th Triennale

1947   8th Triennale

1951   9th Triennale

1954   10th Triennale

1957   11th Triennale

1960   12th Triennale

1964   13th Triennale

1968   14th Triennale

1988   17th Triennale

1992   *Italia Triennale of Milan International Exhibition of the 18th Triennale*

1996   *Italia Triennale of Milan*

INDEX